Copyright © MCMLXXVIII by British Broadcasting Corporation
All rights reserved throughout the world.
Published in Great Britain by World Distributors (Manchester) Limited.
A Pentos Company. P.O. Box 111, 12 Lever Street, Manchester M60 1TS,
by arrangement with the British Broadcasting Corporation.
Printed in Italy.
SBN 7235 6519 8

£1.50

MY MATCH OF THE DAY

BY MIKE CHANNON

It shouldn't be too hard for any keen student of football to guess the game rated by Mike Channon as his Most Memorable *Match of the Day*.

"In fact," says Mike, "it probably only just qualifies because it was a 'Cup Final Match of the Day', not a regular programme.

"I didn't even see it either —at least not at the time. It was when I was with Southampton and we won the Cup, just about the greatest day in my football life.

"The game was shown live, of course, and the same evening the highlights were introduced from our celebration party. So even though I, and all the lads, were in the programme, we couldn't actually see it. But I cheated a bit and arranged for a friend to record both the match and the programme in the evening on a video tape recording machine I had just acquired.

"Some people reckoned the game fell short of being a classic, but I would ask them to remember that for any side in a cup final the priority is to win. Attractive football is the ideal, but there's nothing

attractive about being a losing finalist.

"I'm not saying that game wasn't a good one. It was simply that we were determined not to let Manchester United settle so that they could do what every so-called expert claimed they would do and overwhelm us Second Division no-hopers.

"The first few minutes were dodgy for us, with the ball bouncing around our goalmouth like a hot potato as Ian Turner struggled to keep it out. But gradually we settled. I wasn't having a great game but I felt that things were going well enough for me to take any chance that might occur.

"After about half an hour I got that chance when Jim McCalliog played a fine ball through the middle which I latched on to and set off for goal. Alex Stepney came off his line and I dummied him the wrong way as I aimed for just inside the right hand post.

"Would you believe it? As Alex dived one way the ball hit his outstretched foot and was scrambled clear.

"After half-time the game settled down and stayed fairly even but, with no goals coming, United began to get anxious. With about twenty minutes to go they made it clear just how worried they were by taking Gordon Hill off and bringing on David McCreery.

"I was disappointed to see Gordon go because he had not been having a very happy time. This meant our plans to keep United quiet on the flanks were working. My concern was that McCreery's arrival might alter the pattern of things.

"But soon after this, as time appeared to be running out, we scored the all-important goal. If you're going to win a game with its only goal, then leave it as late as you can to score. The later it is, the less time there is for the other side to equalise.

"Well, with just seven minutes to go, Jim McCalliog sent yet another beautifully weighted ball high through the middle, this time for Bobby Stokes to run on to. Bobby hit the ball very early with his left foot and it went past Stepney's outstretched left hand into the corner of the net!

For the rest of the game it was just a question of willing the clock to tick as fast as possible until Clive Thomas blew his whistle and I realised my great ambition . . . an F.A. Cup winner's medal.

Match of the Day Verdict: Mike Channon's memory—and his video recorder—serve him well. As he says, Saints were rank outsiders who were expected to be over-run by United, especially down the wings. But manager Lawrie Mc-Menemy had clearly planned his strategy well and, after a few shocks, Saints settled to match United all the way. Channon's recall of his 33rd minute near-miss is accurate. Although he did not have an outstanding game by his own standards, he posed a constant threat with his pace and

willingness to run at opponents. His version of the winning goal corresponds with the experts' verdict at the time. Stokes clearly gained an advantage by striking the ball as soon as possible, thus preventing Alex Stepney from anticipating what he might do.

Match of the Day Facts: F.A. Cup Final, Saturday, May 1, 1976. Venue—Wembley. Manchester United 0 Southampton 1.

BY TREVOR FRANCIS

Having played with Birmingham for all my professional career we have not figured that often in *Match of the Day*.

So when the opportunity comes along it is vitally important to try and do reasonably well in front of the cameras. It is amazing how people remember you if you have a good game on *Match of the Day*.

You can play brilliantly week in and week out without getting a lot of recognition—but if you turn it on while the cameras are watching, everyone in soccer knows about it.

It must also help your career internationally. England manager Ron Greenwood is more likely to go and watch a match between the two top teams where he can look at seven or eight England possibilities than watch a game involving only a couple of international-class players.

You hope though that you do enough on television to persuade him to come and watch you.

There are a couple of games that meant a lot to me. The first was against Queen's Park Rangers in 1976–77 when Jimmy Hill did a comparison between myself and Stan Bowles, who was playing particularly well at the time.

I made the first goal for Kenny Burns and scored the second—a goal which eventually was placed runner-up

in the Goal of the Season competition.

I remember I got the ball from a throw in on the left and turned on somebody, beat a couple of players, came across the box and hit it on my left foot past Phil Parkes. It was good to see it later that night.

The same season there was also another memorable game—when we beat Leicester 6-2 away. I scored a goal that went on to win the Goal of the Month Competition.

If you score goals in *Match of the Day* you find that people are always talking about them far more than if it was a game without the cameras.

Match of the Day Verdict: "It took a tremendous chip shot in the F.A. Cup semi-final from Liverpool's Terry McDermott to stop Trevor Francis' goal taking the season's top prize. Even then it was a very close run thing."

Match of the Day Facts: Birmingham City v Queen's Park Rangers, Football League, Division One, Saturday, October 30, 1976.

BY JIM BLYTH

Without a doubt the match I'll always remember was last season's game against Liverpool.

The Scotland World Cup squad had been announced in the week and I was in it. That geed me up a little bit for the Saturday.

We started off the match quite well, but midway through the first half we lost Donato Nardiello off the wing. About a minute later Ray Graydon pulled up with a hamstring, and we virtually played with ten men for the rest of the game.

Liverpool had a lot of the attack and they threw everything at me. They even got a penalty and I stopped that. Then we broke away and scored and won 1-0.

I think you are a bit more worried about making a mistake on *Match of the Day*, because once you make a mistake in front of the cameras it's there for all time.

When you've had a game like I did against Liverpool you get lots of people you don't know passing you by in the street and saying 'well done'.

There are two saves in par-

ticular that I'll remember. One was the penalty from Phil Neal, because he doesn't miss many.

The other came when David Fairclough cut in once from the right and hit an inswinger towards the corner of the net.

I managed to get a finger to it and touched it onto the bar and over. That was probably the best save I made all game—a match I'll always remember as my *Match of the Day*.

Match of the Day Verdict: "It was a display of goalkeeping as good as any we have had on the programme. Pat Jennings and Peter Bonetti have turned in some marvellous performances over the year but this was as good as any.

"It was a match that must have impressed Scottish team manager Ally McLeod that he was absolutely right in picking Jim in his World Cup squad."

Match of the Day Facts: Coventry v Liverpool, Football League, Division One, Saturday, February 4, 1978.

BY COLIN LEE

At first I wasn't going to play in the game against Bristol Rovers because Spurs were going to put me in the reserves.

But there were a lot of injuries and I virtually had to play. At the time I was still nursing an achilles tendon so I wasn't properly fit myself.

I'd trained with Torquay United on the Monday and the Tuesday, travelled to London on the Wednesday and signed for Spurs on the Thursday. When I signed everyone else was at the training ground in Hertfordshire, so when I arrived at White Hart Lane for the match I didn't know half the lads.

I'd not even trained with them!

The game just went fantastic. Everything seemed to go right for us on the day. I can't remember a great deal about the game itself, although a supporter taped *Match of the Day* and gave me it as a souvenir.

I don't have a recording machine myself, but I have a friend who has one and we've watched it a couple of times. It's unbelievable.

I had been used to playing in front of 2,500 people and then I went out in front of 27,000—and millions watching on television.

I just thought I'd go out and play my normal game. When I scored my first that was fantastic—and everything just went better and better.

On the Sunday I went back to my home in Devon and the telephone never stopped ringing. I had to leave it off the hook so that my wife and I could get something to eat!

It was a different world. Suddenly I was front page news everywhere, with photographers coming along to the house.

I had been with Bristol City before joining Torquay so I knew some of the Rovers players—but not the goalkeeper Glyn Jones. At the end of the match he gave me

a smile and we've met since.

We don't talk about the match except maybe to have a laugh about it. Having watched the recording of the game I know now that he made some fantastic saves—we could have got more than nine but for him.

The second goal is the one I remember—it was a corner from the left hand side and I got up and nodded it in. I think that was the best of the four I scored.

Match of the Day Verdict: "The same day we were covering the Merseyside derby which has a reputation for producing goalless draws, so we looked down the fixtures for a match that we thought might give us a few goals and the one we chose was Spurs v Bristol Rovers.

"But we never dreamt it would end the way it did—with the biggest ever *Match of the Day* **score and a four-goal debut from Colin Lee. Overnight he became the talk of soccer."**

Match of the Day Facts: Tottenham Hotspur v Bristol Rovers, Football League Division Two, Saturday, October 22, 1977.

by BRIAN LITTLE

Brian Little, Aston Villa's sparkling England forward, hasn't found *Match of the Day* a particularly happy hunting ground: "I've had some pretty good games that have been televised," he hastens to assure people. "It's just that they have either been in mid-week or on the other channel."

The Durham-born star who began with Aston Villa as an apprentice and signed professional forms in February 1971 had a fine start to his League career. He scored on his debut against Torquay United in April 1972. "That one definitely wasn't on *Match of the Day*," he laughs. "I suppose one of the games which was on the programme which comes immediately to my mind was the 6th round F.A. Cup game against Manchester United at Old Trafford in 1977. The atmosphere was quite fantastic, with almost 60,000 fans packed into the ground. I recall that very early in the game I picked up a ball in mid-field; it must have been somewhere very near the half-way line.

"Anyway, as soon as I got the ball I looked around for support, but there was nobody near me . . . only defenders. The only thing I could do was to go at them.

"I was about 30 yards or so out, and there was still no support. All I could do was have a go at goal. So I had a swing. I connected beautifully and the ball went like a rocket into the back of the net.

"I was delighted, of course, and a bit surprised because I don't often score from any

sort of distance out. I tend to do most of my good work in the box where I can snaffle up any half-chances."

Brian is a regular *Match of the Day* viewer: "I stay in to watch on most Saturday evenings," he says, "assuming I'm not travelling back from a game. I don't really watch to learn anything. I just look in because it's entertaining.

"I don't watch defenders to try and work out ways I can beat them. No, I like to watch the forwards closely and if any of them do something that's a bit clever or different I think—I'll try that next week. I often do too!

"Trevor Francis and Dennis Tueart are the sort of players I enjoy watching. They're skilful players who are prepared to try and do things that are different and perhaps difficult. I don't watch the forwards just because I'm one myself. I think they provide most of the entertainment. Next time you're coming away from a match, think back to all the moments you enjoyed the most. I bet it's the forwards you remember. Good defensive play is one thing, but it's clever, attacking skills that people really love to see."

Match of the Day Verdict: Brian Little's goal was a magnificent piece of skill that really set the game alight. United were stung into furious retaliation and Villa, without injured striker Andy Gray, were forced to defend for long periods.

Match of the Day Facts: Manchester United 2 Aston Villa 1. F.A. Cup 6th Round, Saturday, March 19, 1977.

NOTTINGHAM FOREST

TEAM OF THE YEAR

Archie Gemmill, the dynamic little Scot who really makes Forest tick in mid-field.

Goalkeeper Peter Shilton, the man voted by his fellow professionals as their Player of the Year, marshals his defence.

Forest's Tony Woodcock, the Professional Footballers' Association's Young Player of the Year, in possession against West Ham.

I t's never easy to pick out a 'Team of the Year'. Every team that wins something probably reckons it has some claims to such a title, and when you remember just how many cups and trophies there are to be won in every football season you begin to appreciate the difficulty of selecting just ONE team as the outstanding side.

Just think back to last season and the way Watford stormed out of Division Four, or how little Wrexham performed in the F.A. Cup. Orient did even better and once again mighty Liverpool proved that there wasn't much wrong with English football at club level with yet another magnificent European Cup campaign.

But from the very start of the season Nottingham Forest were extra special. Inspired by the Brian Clough/Peter Taylor managerial partnership, the team which had just managed to claw its way out of the Second Division the previous season set the League Championship chase alight. For the first half of the season all the pundits were confidently assuring us that it was only a matter of time before Cloughie's men 'blew up' and the established favourites took over at the top of the table.

But Clough and Taylor had done it all before, at Derby County, and as the season reached its final run-in stage and Forest were still riding high, the media 'experts' began to accept the team for what it is . . . one of the most attractive, positive footballing sides to emerge in recent years. As late as March the team was still in the hunt for the unique treble of League Championship, F.A. Cup and League Cup.

From left to right it's Viv Anderson, David Needham, Kenny Burns and Archie Gemmill. The lone Norwich City man is Martin Peters.

They didn't make it in the F.A. Cup but did manage to snatch the League Cup in a dramatic 1-0 replay victory over Liverpool. They still get our vote for the 'Team of the Year' and here are some examples of that typical Forest footballing style.

David Needham (No. 5) gets up well above Trevor Brooking and his West Ham team mates.

Defenders and attackers of both sides are involved as Forest bid to repel this assault on their goal.

SCOTLAND THE BRAVE

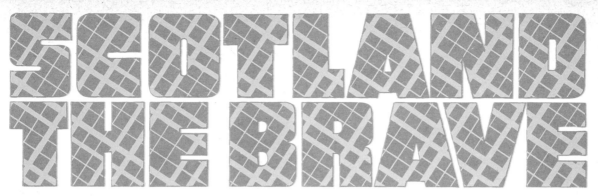

To viewers elsewhere in Britain, Scottish soccer 'on the box' may only be confined to a few brief seconds on a Saturday lunchtime, with footage usually showing some unfortunate 'keeper or other fumbling a vital cross—with only the biennial lesson handed out at Wembley to bring home the fact that Scotland maintains a solid reputation of real skill at her national game.

A Saturday night north of the border also revolves around the ten o'clock telespot however, with wives, sisters and sweethearts packed off to the kitchen to prepare supper as fathers and sons gather to view the day's events and provide armchair criticism of pithy wit as the programme and games unfold.

Presented for the past few years by Archie MacPherson, a man with hair resembling rusty steel wool and a sharp eye for soccer detail, BBC Scotland's *Sportscene* has ruled Saturday suppertimes in Scotland for many years—until 1974 the programme was called *Sportsreel*—and a set format has been established.

Brief introductions from former schoolteacher Archie, fifteen minutes or so from the chosen Premier League fixture of the afternoon, a further brief chat before the odd snatch from a rugby international or other non-soccer sporting event that *Grandstand* cameras might have conveniently collected during the day, and then ten minutes from the preferred English match out of *Match of the Day*'s clutch for the night.

To aid MacPherson and back-up man Gordon Hewitt (a highly-qualified economist, who holds an important post at Edinburgh's Heriot-Watt University when not introducing a variety of sporting programmes for BBC Scotland), commentaries are usually provided by the experienced Alastair Alexander.

Sportscene's ancestry can be traced back to March 20th 1958, when the very first *Sportsreel* programme was presented by the late Peter Thompson, long-time radio veteran of BBC Scotland's squad—and in these days it was a shaky twenty minutes of hit-or-miss television that the country's watchers tuned into! All the matches had to be filmed in these days, long before video-taping became commonplace, and stories of the wrong sequence of reels being shown to a puzzled audience can still raise temperatures a little around BBC headquarters, even today! Since then, techniques have improved out of sight, and soccer has become the Saturday-night staple diet each winter ever since.

By *Match of the Day* standards, the Scottish productions may lack just a little of the sophistication of the south—although football fans north of the border would probably claim that the soccer itself was of such a high standard, production failings go un-noticed! To a degree, this can be traced to simple economics—BBC Scotland cannot yet spare more than three cameras for the regular Saturday games, and in fact there are few Scottish grounds at which more than three cameras could often be employed to any great advantage.

Slow-motion replays—such a feature of *Match of the Day* talk-ins—are as yet unknown in the north—for the simple reason that the BBC's only slow-motion replay unit is safely locked up in London!

Not only the fans watch *Sportscene* of

course—Scotland's biggest fan of all, team boss Ally McLeod, is a confirmed television addict where soccer is concerned and has been known to assert that his specific interest in some Anglo-Scottish stars has first been raised by his having caught their performance on the night that an English game in which they featured was covered by the programme. A great many players watch as well, and several rising Scottish stars will readily admit to having carefully noted several gambits from televised matches that they might not have wholly appreciated from playing at ground level!

And to have been able to see the formative skills of players like Lou Macari and Kenny Dalglish—both now settled into First Division soccer over the border—must have provided expert tuition to many a lad from the slums of Glasgow or the Highlands of the North.

If Scottish viewers have a regular complaint about televised soccer, it could be a decided exclusion of Scottish action from the occasional 'Goal of the Week/Month/Year/ Decade' contests that are screened from London—don't the powers-that-be bother to look at BBC Scotland's clippings? Certainly the standard of play in Scotland is at a higher-than-ever level these days—recent World Cup qualifications must surely underline that point, sore as it may be to English readers—and the goals (or even the saves, despite those occasional lunchtime pundits we keep seeing arguing otherwise) that are produced by the *Sportscene* cameras should by rights get a chance of inclusion in these listings from time to time.

The new heights that Scottish soccer is currently scaling can in the main be traced back to the unusual foresight of Scottish League officials, who pressed ahead with reorganization three years ago in the face of some criticism, and introduced the country's Premier League, which (backed up by the First and Second Divisions comprising another 28 clubs) has in three short seasons surely become the tightest ten-team tourney in Europe! If the competition now means that even the mightiest have to occasionally worry about the odd hint of relegation—as the normally all-powerful Celtic must have done at times last season—then this is no bad thing.

In the eyes of *Sportscene* watchers, Premier League football means good viewing. Close, flinty combat every week, with every club having something to play for in every match. This means that the programme's controllers

can be safe in their choice of match (although their choice appears to include the Rangers or Celtic fixture of the day more often than chance might suggest it should) these days—much more so than in the old pre-Premier days, when after Christmas there were too often too many meaningless fixtures around.

Where and how else does *Sportscene* differ from the current *Match of the Day* programmes? Apart from the time difference, the Scots tend to see more filmed action and less chatter and analysis than is usual to the south of Hadrian's Wall—but with two matches to be shown and the day's results to be looked over and discussed briefly all in that half-hour, this is not surprising. The presenters, especially MacPherson, are more homespun than the London crew, yet their knowledge is no less for that, as Archie's regular engagement to provide a Scottish commentary on all important internationals will disclose. Which brings us to a perhaps little-known point—when Scottish and English viewers are sharing a match such as a World Cup encounter or perhaps the annual Scotland/England climax to the Home International Championship, two different commentators are provided to add the words to BBC pictures—MacPherson to talk to the Scots, while one of the *Match of the Day* team does the speaking for English viewers!

To produce *Sportscene* requires as great a team effort as would be required to win the Premier League! While Archie MacPherson—who was at one time the youngest headmaster of any school in Scotland, and who drifted into broadcasting as a result of his being asked to provide a few scripts for schools broadcasts some years ago—faces the cameras in the studio on a Saturday evening, he is fronting an operation that requires a squad of 24! Eight

floor workers in the studio and another eight up in the control gallery tie in with half-a-dozen more technicians on duty in the video room—and of course the main purpose of the studio team is to present the pictures obtained during the day's game by a further eighteen or so tireless workers at the matches, manning cameras, microphones and control units!

The sum total of the whole effort is what matters, and when MacPherson fronts his show with all the authority that he is reputed to have used as a centre-half of some distinction in junior football a few years ago, the end result is one in which Scotland's sporting public are justly satisfied—and if you can satisfy Scotland's sporting public, then you can be sure that you're doing a good job!

GOALS OF THE SEASONS

1970–71

Scorer: Ernie Hunt (Coventry City). Match: Coventry City v Everton, Football League, Division One, Highfield Road, Coventry, Saturday, October 3, 1970.

ACTION REPLAY: The goal that won the first ever Goal of the Season competition—and a score that will NEVER be repeated. For the free-kick move that produced the goal was subsequently outlawed by the football authorities. Coventry won a free kick only a foot outside the penalty area but brought the ball back a yard or so. Willie Carr stood over the ball and alongside him three Coventry players—Brian Alderson, Dave Clements and Ernie Hunt. Everton put up a four man wall with a fifth defender marking a Coventry forward on the edge of the defensive barrier. Carr, standing over the ball, flicked it

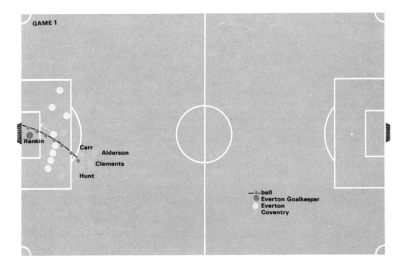

up with his heels and Hunt volleyed home a right foot shot without the ball ever touching the ground. At a later date it was ruled that the move was in contravention of rule 13 which states that at a free kick the ball shall be in play when it has travelled the distance of its own circumference.

1971–72

Scorer: Ron Radford (Hereford United). Match: Hereford United v Newcastle United, F.A. Cup Third Round Replay, Edgar Street Athletic Ground, Hereford, Saturday, February 5, 1972.

ACTION REPLAY: When the time comes for a 'goal of the century' then Ronnie Radford will have a justifiable claim. For other than the sheer mechanics of the goal itself it was historic in that it not only helped non-league Hereford dismiss First Division opponents Newcastle but it also brought the little club to the notice of the world—and probably played a major part in having them elected to the Football League at the end of the season. The goal itself began and ended with Radford. He won a tackle inside the Newcastle half and moved forward before hitting the ball to full-back George Griffiths who was tightly marked by a Newcastle

defender. Griffiths instantly laid the ball back into Radford's path and from fully 35 yards he hit a left foot shot that cleared the defenders to put Hereford on the road to victory. The game was played on a Saturday afternoon—the same day as most other clubs were engaged in Fourth Round ties after Hereford had drawn 2–2 at Newcastle in the first game.

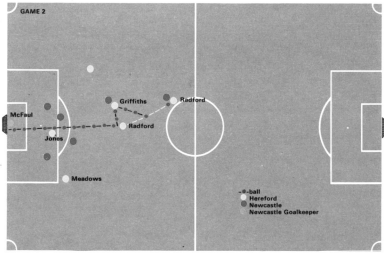

1972–73

Scorer: Peter Osgood (Chelsea). Match: Chelsea v Arsenal, F.A. Cup Sixth Round, Stamford Bridge, London, Saturday, March 17, 1973.

ACTION REPLAY: A goal that had commentator David Coleman saying: "You don't blame goalkeepers for goals like that—you praise the scorer." The move originated ten yards inside the Arsenal half with Alan Hudson pushing the ball out to his right where full-back Gary Locke was beginning a run. Locke moved forward 20 yards before crossing. Peter Osgood—on the edge of the penalty circle—outjumped his marking defender to head the ball into the box where Steve Kember (Chelsea) and Eddie Kelly challenged for the ball. It broke to Osgood, still outside the area, who rifled home a left foot shot that whistled past Bob Wilson's right shoulder.

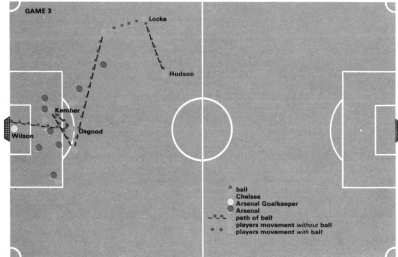

1973–74

Scorer: Alan Mullery (Fulham).
Match: Fulham v Leicester City, F.A. Cup Fourth Round, Craven Cottage, London, Saturday, January 26, 1974.

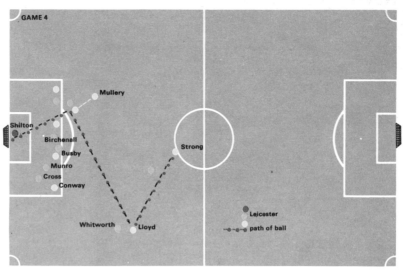

1974–75

Scorer: Mick Walsh (Blackpool). **Match:** Blackpool v Sunderland, Football League Division Two, Bloomfield Road, Blackpool, Saturday, February 1, 1975.

ACTION REPLAY: A superb solo goal. Sunderland were attacking down the right flank and a long cross ball was headed out of defence by Blackpool's Bob Hatton to Paul Hart, some yards outside the penalty circle.

ACTION REPLAY: Fulham's Les Strong collected a ball on the edge of the centre circle just inside the Leicester half and threaded a ball out to his left wing for Barry Lloyd whose cross was met, on the volley, by He hit a long ball to the centre circle where Mick Walsh brought the ball down on his chest and set off on a long run deep into Sunderland territory. On the edge of the penalty area his only ball looked to be a crossfield pass to either Alan Ainscow or Wyn Davies, both square. Instead he checked, turned inside and hit a glorious swerving left foot shot from the edge of the area around defender Bobby Moncur and beyond goalkeeper Jim Montgomery.

Alan Mullery, standing on the edge of the penalty circle. Mullery's right foot screamer flew past Peter Shilton in the Leicester goal, giving Fulham a 1–1 draw. They lost the replay 2–1 in extra time.

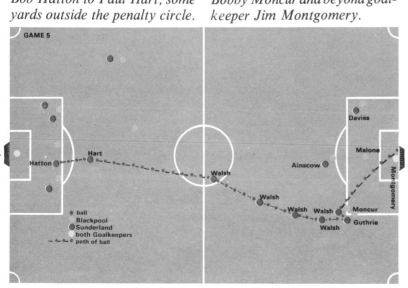

NOTE: Colours used are to aid easy identification and NOT necessarily colours worn by club in these particular matches.

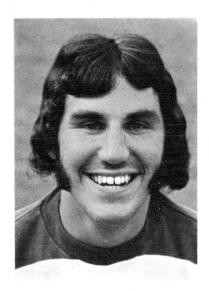

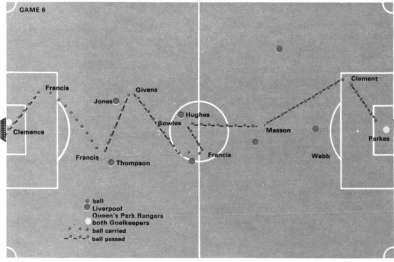

GAME 6

Francis · Givens · Clement · Jones · Hughes · Bowles · Masson · Clemence · Francis · Parkes · Francis · Thompson · Webb

- ● ball
- ● Liverpool
- ● Queen's Park Rangers
- ○ both Goalkeepers
- ◦ ◦ ball carried
- –◦– ◦– ball passed

1975–76

Scorer: Gerry Francis (Queen's Park Rangers). Match: Queen's Park Rangers v Liverpool, Football League Division One, Loftus Road, London, Saturday, August 16, 1975.
ACTION REPLAY: The first Saturday of a new season and a marvellous goal to kick off the new campaign. Queen's Park Rangers goalkeeper Phil Parkes started the move by giving the ball to Dave Clement on the edge of his own penalty area. He stroked the ball to Don Masson in space in the middle of his own half. His foraging ball found Stan Bowles in the centre circle and he cleverly flicked the ball square to Gerry Francis, also on the half way line. Fran- *cis played a one-two with Don Givens and picked up the return outside the Liverpool area. He ran diagonally to his right before hitting a right foot shot across the advancing Ray Clemence (Liverpool). The move took only seconds—and a Liverpool player never touched the ball once it left Phil Parkes' hands in the Queen's Park Rangers goal.*

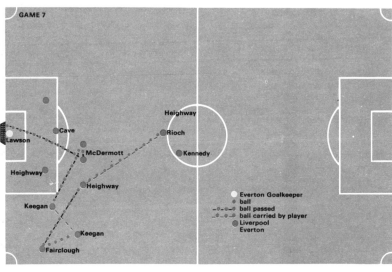

GAME 7

Heighway · Cave · Rioch · McDermott · Kennedy · Lawson · Heighway · Heighway · Keegan · Keegan · Fairclough

- ○ Everton Goalkeeper
- ● ball
- –◦– ◦– ball passed
- –◦– ◦– ball carried by player
- ● Liverpool
- ● Everton

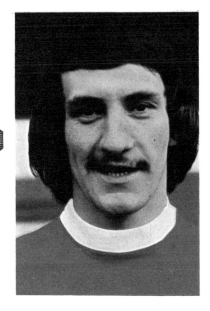

1976–77

Scorer: Terry McDermott (Liverpool). Match: Everton v Liverpool, F.A. Cup Semi-final, Maine Road, Manchester, Saturday, April 23, 1977.
ACTION REPLAY: Ray Kennedy (Liverpool) won a tackle on the edge of the centre circle against Bruce Rioch (Everton). Liverpool's Steve Heighway picked up the ball and went on a diagonal run towards the corner of the penalty area before pushing the ball out to David Fairclough lying wide on the left. He gave the ball straight to Kevin Keegan, who moved towards the edge of the area before pass- *ing the ball back to Terry McDermott, some five yards outside the box. He sidestepped a challenge, looked up and noticed Everton goalkeeper David Lawson off his line. His left foot chip shot cleared Lawson to give Liverpool a lead.*

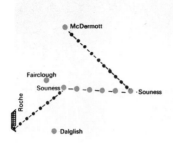

McDermott

Fairclough

Souness

Roche

Souness

Dalglish

- ● Liverpool
  Manchester United
  goalkeeper
- ● ball
- -●-● path of ball
- -●--● playing moving

1977 - 78

Scorer: Graeme Souness (Liverpool). Match: Liverpool v Manchester United, Football League, Division One, Anfield, Liverpool, Saturday, February 25, 1978.

ACTION REPLAY: A memorable goal for more than one reason. Not only was it a perfect example of the volley but it was Graeme Souness' first goal for his new club following his transfer from Middlesbrough. He played his part in the build-up by spraying the ball from the middle of the park to midfield partner Terry McDermott wide on the right wing. With both Liverpool and Manchester United players funnelling back into the penalty area McDermott floated across a centre that Souness met on the volley with a left foot shot that left Paddy Roche helpless in the United goal. The sheer pace of Souness' left foot shot was, in itself, worthy of the accolade Goal of the Season—one of three scored by Liverpool players that qualified for the final six.

DAVID COLEMAN

The role of the commentator is that of an unbiased observer—trying to please most of the people most of the time. But even the men behind the mikes have their own personal favourites—although it would be hard to link the right club with the right commentator.

David Coleman though will readily admit that he has a soft spot for ... Stockport County! Little wonder. For one of the background facts thrown up by research into David's own sporting background reveals that he actually played for the Cheshire club!

It was back in the early fifties when he made a couple of appearances for his local team. Not in the Football League, mind you—but for Stockport County reserves.

But journalism held far more sway with the youthful Coleman than a career in soccer and his footballing days soon ended when he began to make progress in the newspaper world.

He began the writing side of his career as a reporter on the *Stockport Express* and later became editor on his local paper as a 22-year-old.

In 1953 he started freelance radio work in Manchester and the following year joined the BBC in Birmingham as a News Assistant, being appointed Sports Editor of the Midland Region in November 1955.

By 1958 he had become a regular television commentator on both soccer and his other sports love, athletics (he was a county class athlete).

During his commentating career David, a married man with six children, has described the scene at numerous major sporting events ranging from

the Olympic Games and World Cup to the Grand National and F.A. Cup Final.

He has also had spells as the front-man on both *Grandstand* and *Sportsnight* which was, at one stage, retitled *Sportsnight with Coleman* before he left the BBC to work abroad.

He returned, of course, in time for the summer's World Cup in Argentina, where he again established himself as the country's number one soccer commentator.

Despite a life that is the envy of millions, one major ambition eluded him—and there now seems little likelihood of him achieving it.

He always wanted to run a four-minute mile!

"When I moved to the BBC Manchester I used to run to the office in my athletics gear and change into a suit when I arrived. You can imagine some of the jokes that were made but it was worth it to keep fit for my work," he has recalled.

That was some twenty years ago—but even today he places great store on physical and mental fitness for his role as *Match of the Day* commentator.

THE DAY WE BOTH MISSED A PUNCH!

Referee Ron Crabb jumped into his car parked outside Highbury to make the high-speed motorway dash to his West Country home.

His target was to have his coat and shoes off and be settled in front of the television set in time for that Saturday evening's *Match of the Day*.

"I thought I'd missed something on the field," Ron explained. "I was in charge of the Arsenal-Sunderland game and it was on *Match of the Day*. As

I was booking a player I sensed that something had happened behind my back by the crowd reaction.

"I didn't know what it was and I asked my linesmen if they had seen anything and they hadn't. I thought that whatever it was the cameras would have picked it up and I would be able to see it that night.

"I got home in time and switched on—but they showed nothing that I hadn't seen and

1 Referee Ron Crabb calls off the Plymouth Argyle–Bradford City Third Division match—the first time in his career he has failed to finish a game he started.

I thought I must have been wrong over my intuition.

"But then on the Monday morning there was a big photograph in one of the morning

papers showing Arsenal's Wilf Rostron throwing a punch at Sunderland's Bobby Kerr. It was a punch that I'd missed—and so had *Match of the Day*!"

While there may be some referees who feel that the replaying of controversial decisions should not be allowed 47-year-old Mr. Crabb, a prison officer who retired from

the Football League list at the end of the 1977–78 season, is an eloquent advocate of *Match of the Day*'s right to discuss important refereeing points.

He is well qualified to speak on the subject as he has been a regular *Match of the Day* man in the middle and was, at one time, the referee who featured on the show's opening credits for a full season.

Said Ron: "I always try and get home in time to watch the programme—and normally I can make it. If it's the match you have been refereeing then obviously you look to see if you have missed anything.

"If you are not involved in the game you can watch it as a game of football, although you do get involved if Jimmy Hill raises any refereeing point. I often think that it is easy to make the decisions when you are up in the stand and have the advantage of a replay but it's far different in the heat of the moment down on the field. On the day I think I would probably have done the same as the referee—even if it was a mistake.

"The game itself though is there for me to enjoy. I just sit back and live it as a game of football. It's different from going to watch a game live. Then I can't seem to get into the game—I'm always watching the referee.

"Television allows me to enjoy the game for what it is— a football match. Maybe it's because if it is a live match you get involved before and after. I'll go into the changing rooms to say hello to the referee and see him for a drink afterwards.

"At home you are more divorced from the man in the middle.

"I don't mind seeing incidents involving me played back on television. I accept that. I have had two particular incidents when I have awarded penalties that were disputed, and each time it's been proved that I was right.

"Last season there was a game at West Ham where there was a bit of doubt about a Malcolm MacDonald goal. I allowed it because the linesman didn't flag—when it comes to offside it is nearly always the linesman who makes the decision rather than the referee— but whether or not that decision was right was never really proved because of the camera angles.

"Had I been wrong it wouldn't have worried me. I have always gone through life with the philosophy that if I make a mistake I will never worry about what people say. This has helped me in refereeing to a certain degree because if I see something on *Match of the Day* it wouldn't bother me. I know there are some referees who get uptight about it—but not me.

"I suppose if you know the cameras are at a match it affects you slightly before the game. Consciously you are aware of this. I say to myself: 'you've got to do that little bit extra because instead of having 20,000 or 40,000 people watching you've got millions.' Maybe it seems to make you that little

2 That's it. Referee Ron Crabb calls it a day after 45 minutes battling against a snowstorm. For Ron the match—Plymouth Argyle v Bradford City—will always be remembered as his Match of the Season. It was the first time he had stopped a game he had started—and the abandonment provided him with the final match of his career when he was put in charge of the re-staged game at the end of the 1977–78 season.

bit more cautious—but pressure-wise it doesn't bother me.

"As for Clinical Jimmy you can't take away from the man. He's been right through the mill—he started off as a player and knows what it's all about. He has a job to do and he's got to present it in a way which will give maximum enjoyment to the viewers.

"I don't know why some referees are upset by television criticism—after all ninety-nine times out of a hundred the referee is proved right.

"If he was in the middle of the park and a bloke in the crowd said he was useless he wouldn't turn round and have a stand-up.

"Spectators pay their money so are entitled to have a shout and the same with television. They pay their money to televise games so it should be entirely up to them to say what they want on the day."

SHORT PASSES

Dorchester Town striker Brian Southern walked down the aisle to the strains of the catchy *Match of the Day* signature tune when he married his sweetheart in 1973. He felt the tune was more appropriate than the conventional wedding marches. . . .

A Derby policeman won't forget the afternoon that the Match of the Day *team covered the Rams' First Division match against Chelsea. While he was sitting at home enjoying the soccer the cameras focused on a terrace fight—and the officer spotted a hooligan kicking and hitting rival fans. He recognised him as a youth he had previously arrested and brought him to justice.*

The *Match of the Day* tune was the work of songwriter Barry Stoller. He wrote it in December 1971—and it's been heard thousands of times since, either on the show itself or at all the league and non-league grounds where it is played seconds before the teams take the field.

Much travelled striker BOBBY GOULD has always been a television favourite—and he revels in his fame as a wit.

When he was playing on the wing for West Ham during a Match of the Day *broadcast from Sheffield he created a new first!*

In those days Brammall Lane was shared by the Blades and Yorkshire county cricket team and the old commentary position was well away from the fans—on the cricket boundary.

Gould had made a run down the flank but was dispossessed—and turned to commentator John Motson inquiring: "Did you get that one!"

* * *

Several teams believe they never give of their best when *Match of the Day* are covering their games. Two Manchester City players, Dennis Tueart and Dave Watson in particular, felt that there was a jinx on City when they were on the box.

* * *

Cardiff referee Mike Thomas is an ardent Match of the Day *statistician. He keeps a permanent record of all matches screened since the show first went on the air.*

The Football League lay down strict rules about *Match of the Day* coverage.

A total of sixty league matches are shown throughout the season and of these at least 18 must come from outside the First Division—fourteen of them from Division Two and the remainder from Divisions Three and Four.

Of these at least half (seven from Division Two and two from the bottom two leagues) must be screened as the main match.

Additionally the B.B.C. cameras have to visit every one of the 22 First Division grounds at least once during the season.

* * *

Match of the Day *fans include the Bishop of Norwich, the Dean of Westminster and the Chinese Ambassador in London.*

There are only sixteen current Football League grounds which *Match of the Day* has not visited.

*   *   *

It was a woman who was responsible for *Match of the Day* including the manager's name in their pre-match team line-up. Mrs. Lilian Bruce from Harrow, Middlesex, wrote asking the production team to do it—and they latched onto her suggestion.

*   *   *

Ex-England full-back Ray Wilson often struck terror into a winger's heart . . . and that of Match of the Day *commentator Ken Wolstenholme.*

Ray was a natural born comic and they still laugh at Goodison about the day he hoaxed Match of the Day.

Ken Wolstenholme was standing outside the dressing rooms about forty-five minutes before the kick-off of a Leeds United–Everton match when Ray came out of the dressing room to go to the toilet.

He spotted Ken putting the team down on paper ready for his commentary. Ray looked over his shoulder and disappeared back into the dressing-room.

A few minutes later Alan Ball appeared—in his street clothes with the exception of Everton's number two jersey.

Over the next fifteen minutes there was a succession of Everton players making tracks for the loo—and each one wearing an unaccustomed number.

Forward Jimmy Husband was number five; winger Johnny Morrissey was number nine; and then—the biggest shock of all—goalkeeper Gordon West walked out with bandages around his head and arms, walking with a limp and the aid of two sticks.

By then Wolstenholme didn't know what was happening and was surrounded by crumpled pieces of paper on which he'd written his updated Everton line-up.

The ruse wasn't blown open until Wilson re-appeared—this time wearing a goalkeeper's jersey that stretched to his knees and a 1928-style Yorkshire cap.

He winked at Ken and inquired: "Have you got problems?"

It was later to transpire that the Toffeeman had deliberately detained manager Harry Catterick in the dressing room while they played the elaborate joke on the Beeb.

FLOOR MANAGER, COMPOSER, GOAL-KEEPER . . . THAT'S CHRIS

Week-ends are a busy time for Chris Lewis. As studio floor manager for both *Grandstand* and *Match of the Day*, every Saturday is, for him, something approaching 14 hours of non-stop work and concentration spiced with up to six hours of live television. And it doesn't end there. He's up early on Sunday mornings to sort out any problems concerning the regular charity soccer matches he helps organise as secretary of the Dennis Waterman XI.

The team, skippered by Chris' old mate from *The Sweeney*, plays on most Sunday afternoons to raise money for needy causes, and quite often when celebrity team members are forced to drop out at the very last minute Chris reckons he becomes something of a needy cause himself! His frequent Sunday morning chore is finding showbiz names ready to step in and keep the team up to strength, never an easy task with time running out. To make matters worse, most footballing personalities already have heavy demands on their time.

Having got the team sorted, with help from Dennis and perhaps one or two other regulars in the side, Chris then has to get himself along to wherever the game is being held because he is the team's goal-keeper.

He's always been a goal-keeper, turning out for King's Lynn as a youngster, and later on Wealdstone. Since it's usually tricky finding personalities willing to play in goal—even Bob Wilson insists on performing out on the field!—Chris has been playing in various showbiz sides for many years, and since he helped Dennis Waterman form his own eleven in 1974 he has been an ever-present.

Another string to the Lewis bow is a musical one. Although he began playing rhythm guitar in various Rock 'n' Roll bands in the early 60s, he has in recent years concentrated on writing music. Many of his compositions are familiar melodies to regular BBC Television sports viewers. In fact Chris and his co-writer once had five of their compositions being used as the opening music for programmes all running at the same time.

Since he started writing music in 1972 Chris, together with his regular partner, has been responsible for the themes of a host of programmes including the Olympic Games, Open Golf, Sunday Cricket, Rugby Special, Wimbledon Tennis, Pro-Celebrity Golf and the 1974 World Cup.

Chris Lewis—because of his bright red hair he is known as the 'plunging carrot'—makes a fine save for the Dennis Waterman XI. Recognise the defender in the picture with Chris? Yes, it's Arsenal manager Terry Neil.

QUIZ

1 Leicester City plunged into the transfer market during 1971 and made three £100,000 signings. All three have been familiar *Match of the Day* figures. Who were they?

2 Ron Saunders has made a success of league managership. For which teams did he turn out as a player?

3 Who scored West Germany's goals in the 1966 World Cup Final?

4 *Match of the Day* ran a 'So You Want to be a Commentator' competition and a famous ex-international footballer was among the finalists. Who was he?

5 How many times did Tommy Docherty (photo 1) play for Scotland?

1

6 The first two teams to appear on *Match of the Day* met in the 1970–71 F.A. Cup Final. What was the final score?

7 Scotland's goals in the 1974 World Cup Finals were scored by players from the same club—who were the players and the club concerned?

8 Hereford United's bid for Football League status was given a *Match of the Day* boost when they knocked out Newcastle in the 1971–72 F.A. Cup. Who eventually beat them? A clue is that the player pictured (2) scored a hat-trick in that game.

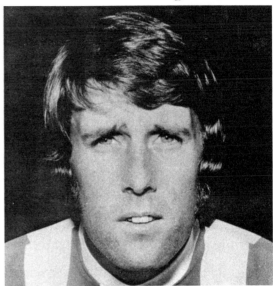

2

9 Millwall hold one unenviable playing record that is unique amongst London's league clubs. What is it?

10 This player (3) figured in one of the biggest transfers of the 1977–78 season. Who is he and between which clubs did he move?

3

11 Who captained Liverpool in the 1974 F.A. Cup Final?

12 Jimmy Greaves scored many marvellous *Match of the Day* goals, but did he score on his debuts for Chelsea, Spurs and England?

13 Who is this Scottish goalkeeper? (photo 4).

4

14 When was the first Charity Shield played? 1901, 1908, 1923 or 1948?
15 Who was England's first international manager?
16 In which season did Ray Wilkins (pictured 5) make his League debut for Chelsea?

5

17 Peter Withe had a spell with South African club Arcadia Shepherds before returning to British soccer to join Wolverhampton Wanderers. But which were his first two Football League clubs?

18 Norman Hunter (photo 6) was a member of England's World Cup squads in both 1966 and 1970. But how many games did he start for England?

6

19 What was Don Masson's first League club?
20 John Richards made his international debut for England in the 1973 Home Internationals. Where was the match played?

Throughout his controversial career the colourful Malcolm Allison has had his critics.

But friends and foes alike all accept that he is one of the leading tacticians of the late sixties and seventies, and his coaching expertise has helped to shape the pattern of play at so many clubs.

And the ex-Manchester City and Crystal Palace manager is the first to admit that television has played a vital part in the development of coaching techniques in recent seasons.

But does constant television exposure destroy a side's qualities of surprise, because all their moves have been seen by millions?

Not according to Allison. He said: "No one had more television than Manchester City in their successful seasons when they won the League Championship and the F.A. Cup.

"The thing about television is that you must use it to help you—and not worry about it. People may say it alerts other teams on set pieces, but as long as you have got alternatives for your set pieces it can be an advantage. At Manchester we used to plan several alternatives so no one knew what was coming when, even if they had seen all the moves before.

"I never felt television was any problem to us. In soccer all clubs watch each other and have reports on teams and players. I couldn't see how *Match of the Day* has any more effect except that a visual thing is more educational than a written report.

"Soccer's a game of copiers and I would watch teams on *Match of the Day*—not so much to find out what they did at free kicks or corners, but to see if they were offering any new alternatives that we could use. I would pick up ideas from other people and it would give us another alternative.

"Probably I could learn more from the foreign programmes because you were watching teams with a different style of play.

"I remember seeing a Spurs game. There was a corner and free kick Spurs used to take. We used to use them abroad more than in England.

MANAGERS

"It was easier to get away with it against foreign opposition.

"Television was more helpful to me in the Second Division, because I didn't know the teams so well. In the First Division I knew them by heart. If a Second Division match was on I would look at it to pick up things.

"The main thing about television is that I would see a player, mainly from the lower divisions, that I felt had something. Maybe I hadn't seen him before or had last seen him as a kid.

"There have been cases where I have seen a player with a lower league team and I hadn't seen him for seven or eight years, and having seen him again on television I would take a closer look, as maybe he could do a job for me.

"It is more pleasure watching *Match of the Day* for a manager, because it's just enjoyment. It's like when he was a player or a kid —it's a relaxation thing to watch when you are not involved."

The greatest asset *Match of the Day* has given Big Mal is to help him demonstrate to players their weaknesses and strengths.

And he often used films of matches to put over this point to players at his various clubs.

Not even top-class internationals like Colin Bell, Mike Summerbee and Tommy Booth were above picking up things from *Match of the Day*.

Continued Allison: "Eight or nine of the Manchester City side used *Match of the Day* to help them. I am a great believer in individual films of players. I think that television could do more for football if they made individual films of players rather than always following the whole match. These films could then be shown to schoolboys—it would be great for the Football Association.

"We would watch games on *Match of the Day*, or go to the studio and watch games if there was something I wanted to stress.

VIEW

Sometimes before certain matches we would watch a particularly good game we had played ourselves to give us a boost.

"I remember playing a European match—it was the quarter final of the European Cup Winners Cup in 1970–71 and we were drawn against the Polish side Gornik.

"We were going to Poland for the first leg and I knew it would be very, very bad freezing weather. So just to show the boys how they could play in bad conditions, I showed them film of a match when we had beaten Spurs in icy conditions.

"We lost the away leg, but still did enough to make sure we got through to the next round by winning the home tie and then beating them 3-1 in a play-off in Copenhagen.

"That particular Manchester City side was one of the best ever to play in icy conditions.

"Two players who improved a lot because of television were Ian Evans and Peter Taylor when they were at Crystal Palace with me.

"They learnt a great deal about their own game. They were young players coming into the side at 20 or 21 so they had many things to improve upon.

"Seeing themselves on *Match of the Day* probably inspired them to work at certain things in training. Ian Evans would watch a good centre half and watch himself and see where he was getting into trouble. Both Taylor and Evans were tremendously improved players over an 18 month period because they watched themselves and other players.

"Visual education is the best, as the Americans say. You can tell a player something in training and ask him to do it, but it isn't until he sees that move on film that he truly realises why it is so important to him."

Over the years Allison built up a reputation for speaking his mind on television—and some of his critics claim that this forthrightness rebounded on his players.

He answers those critics: "When you get an outspoken manager such as Brian Clough or Jackie Charlton I don't believe it puts any extra pressure on the players. In fact I believe the opposite. It puts a certain amount of pressure on the person speaking out but at the same time the pressure is taken off the players.

"Some players used to think differently, but I have always felt it was the correct thing to do. I have said things on *Match of the Day* as psychology—either to build up my own players or frighten the opposition.

"I remember I dropped Mike Doyle and he made some statement about why he was dropped.

"He thought I was picking on him. I later made a statement saying I'd dropped much better players than him. All the lads in the dressing room were laughing, and Mike began to say he had never said the things that had been reported.

"That was an example where I used the media to my advantage with a player.

Lawrie McMenemy, Southampton's bluff Geordie boss, has some close connections with *Match of the Day* and makes no secret of the fact that he enjoys the programme and why: "Football is a family entertainment and *Match of the Day* is a family programme. It has everything a good television plot needs . . . drama, suspense, excitement and plenty of colourful action. It has heroes, villains and even a man to uphold justice. With these ingredients it has got to be a winner."

As one of the judges of the Goal of the Month competition, it could be claimed that Lawrie is slightly biased in the programme's favour, but he'll have none of that. "It's just a question of what people like," he claims. "Whilst I can't say that every family in the land has somebody in it who actually goes to a match each week, I do believe that

25

most families have at least one member who is sufficiently interested to watch it if it is on television. Once you switch on, it's compulsive viewing."

"If you're at a party on a Saturday night you can just about guarantee that if you sneak off to find another room with a television set in it at about 10 o'clock, you won't be alone for long. It isn't anti-social to leave the main party. It seems completely natural and as often as not it ends up with more people watching television than not watching!"

While Lawrie clearly rates *Match of the Day* highly as an entertainment, he doesn't really think it has a great deal to offer the professionals who watch. "From our point of view the programme has some advantages and some disadvantages. It really depends on whether your own team is involved or not. If you see a clever new tactic used by another team, then that's great . . . but if it is your own side's new trick which is exposed to every manager and coach in the game, then that is not so good, I suppose.

"It's a bit like a comedian who works the theatre for years with a first class act. Everywhere he goes he has a new audience and to them his jokes are fresh and funny. But after just one television appearance in front of millions, his jokes become old hat, and before he can carry on working he has to come up with something new.

"But, in fact, I believe the programme is only useful to people who are in the game in a fairly general way. I find I can assess which players are in form and which ones are having a wee bit of a struggle to get the ball to run for them. This can be of some use if you're playing that team in the next week or so.

"Football on television provides the opportunity to have a look at teams and players from divisions other than your own, but I'm doubtful about any specific advantages that managers and players can gain from watching. Goalkeepers obviously like to study penalties being taken and, of course,

we can all learn a little about a team's technique for certain free-kicks.

"The only thing is, you can come awfully unstuck if you take too much notice, because the kick itself isn't that significant. It is the way it is executed that matters and while I suppose there is some advantage in being half ready for what might happen, there's the danger that the opposition might play a double bluff on you, often more by accident than design. You may be all ready for them to work the trick you saw them use on *Match of the Day* the previous week, and then they leave you flat-footed by doing something totally different. Your bit of snooping really back-fires on you then!

"Although I don't think there is too much to be gained from watching other teams on the box, I *do* believe there are tremendous benefits in seeing your own lads in action, both as a team and individually.

"First of all, because you see the game some five hours or so after the final whistle, you are able to view it rather more dispassionately than you could during the on-the-spot excitement at the time. You can see more easily why things went wrong for your side. You have a far better balanced view of the game, enabling you to judge players and issues more fairly.

"Also, because you have a pretty good idea of what is going to happen next, you are able to assess more clearly what should have been done by your own players, either to prevent the opposition from doing something or to ensure that a move is continued and perhaps an attack pressed home by your own team.

"Television is great for coaching. Ten seconds on *Match of the Day* can say more than 1,000 words. If you have a player who is persistently doing something wrong but won't accept that he is at fault, the best way to put it right is for him to see himself on the box. His coach and manager could have spent hours failing to convince him, but a sight of himself actually making his mistake is usually all that is

needed."

Many fans are perhaps curious about whether or not players enjoy being on television or if they would prefer to avoid coming under the all-seeing electronic eye and having their performance analysed. Lawrie agrees that there are perhaps some mixed feelings within the game about the joys of being on television, but he does point out that perhaps we should not take too seriously any players who claim that they would prefer their games not to be screened.

"There are some people in the game who tend to become a bit blasé about being on *Match of the Day*," he says. "They remind me of my National Service days in the Guards. Then there used to be a big moan about duty at Buckingham Palace. 'Oh, not walking about up there again' lots of the lads used to complain. But when they actually got there, all togged up in those beautiful uniforms, marching up and down in front of the crowds, they all used to love it. Well, footballers are like that with *Match of the Day*. Whatever they might say, most of them love to be on it!

"In fact it has some strange effects on some players. Lads in the Southampton team do things in a televised match they would never bother with normally. All this about secret signs for corner kicks and free kicks. Now there are only a few planned variations for a corner kick and seeing that we go over and over everything time and time again in training, there shouldn't be any doubt in any player's mind about what we are going to try and do. And yet, now and again when the cameras have been at one of our games, I've been amazed to see lads in my own team making extraordinary signs in a blatantly obvious way just as they have been about to take a kick. It's quite incredible. The signs don't mean a thing, either to me or anyone in the Saints team. I suppose the lad hopes that if we score then his sign will look good on *Match of the Day* and be carefully analysed and explained to twelve million people by Jimmy Hill!

Switched on Fans...

Eric Morecambe—the footballing half of ITV's Morecambe and Wise—is vice-president of Second Division Luton Town and a loyal *Match of the Day* fan as he reveals here:

"I always watch *Match of the Day*—every Sunday afternoon!

"Officially it's in my ITV contract that I've got to watch Star Soccer or the Big Match—but unofficially I sneak a look at Jimmy Hill. The last time I saw anything like that on Jimmy Hill's chin the whole herd had to be destroyed.

"I've got my own club Luton Town on tape from a *Match of the Day* when they beat Leeds United in the First Division. When we lose I go back and play the ones when we are winning. I've got about four. . . .

"Seriously I'm a big fan of *Match of the Day* and these days I also follow Nottingham Forest. I like Brian Clough—he's a personal friend and it's good to see a team like that doing so well. Apart from Gemmill and Shilton it's a team without names. It's marvellous to see players like Withe and Robertson doing so well—Luton played against them in the Second Division and now they are big stars. It's nice to see that and it's jolly good for the game. It's a change to see Nottingham Forest up there with Manchester United, Liverpool and Everton.

Comedian and singer Don MacLean—still remembered as one of the stars of BBC TV's Crackerjack children's series and a regular guest on ATV's Celebrity Squares—says:

"Being in pantomime every winter I don't get the chance to go along and see my favourite team Birmingham City as often as I would like.

"So most of my football comes from *Match of the Day*. I spend most of December, January and February in panto but I always take along my nine inch black and white portable television for my dressing room.

"Last Christmas there were a bunch of us in panto at Bournemouth—all of us football fans. Lennie Henry supports West Bromwich Albion, Paul and Barry Harman were keen Rotherham fans, and I was for Birmingham.

"One night a party of the West Bromwich footballers came down to the show so we had our own *Match of the Day* afterwards!

"I like the interviews as I'm always interested to hear what the players and managers thought about the game. But the one interview I'll never forget was one with Cyrille Regis.

"It was marvellous. He was asked what was the main difference between playing non-league and playing in the First Division, and his answer was that his mum didn't have to wash his dirty shirts and shorts!"

David Hamilton, one of Radio Two's most popular disc jockeys, reveals:

"If I'm ever feeling low I take out of my collection a very special video cassette.

"It is the *Match of the Day* coverage of the 1975 F.A. Cup Final between Fulham and West Ham. Even though my favourite club Fulham lost they had waited 100 years to get to the Cup Final and that was a proud moment.

"I had followed them right through the rounds to Wembley.

A group of friends and I chartered a plane to fly us up to Carlisle, then to Sheffield for the semi-final and then to Manchester for the replay before we got to Wembley.

"I look at the cassette every few months and one of the things that strikes me is that of the Cup team there are only three still left at Craven Cottage.

"One of the reasons I bought myself a video-tape recorder was so that I wouldn't miss *Match of the Day*.

"Usually I am out working at a

gig on a Saturday night and while I do try and get to a television set it isn't always possible. In that case I make sure I pre-set the video so that it records *Match of the Day*, and I can watch it next day.

"Kathy isn't particularly keen on football and sometimes she wants to watch a film while *Match of the Day* is on, so the video comes in useful and prevents any family disputes!

"I can record it while we watch an old film—and still see all the goals the following morning."

Author Jack Higgins, who wrote the best-selling novel The Eagle Has Landed, is now a tax exile in the Channel Islands—but he's still an ardent *Match of the Day* viewer.

He said: "Over here in such a small place—there's only 75,000—it is obvious that the football is really amateur club standard with gates of 800 to 900 people, so that it's a good example of how fans would be lost without *Match of the Day*.

"You tend to find there are people who are supporters of the

various obvious teams. Obviously from my point of view for years I was interested in what was happening to Leeds United as I lived in Leeds.

"I used to watch them at one time but the depressing thing that put me off in the end was the decline in crowd standards. I had a friend at the time who had gone for years and got a brick in the back of the head. I stopped going after that.

"Nowadays I go to the odd local match and mainly the F.A. Cup Final if I happen to be over. The last time was more than two years

ago.

"I'm a prime example of where television really does a valuable and real service. If it weren't for *Match of the Day* I wouldn't get any real football, there's no doubt about that.

"Football's a kind of theatre of life and drama. I am a great one for football drama—I watch week by week as the Brian Clough story unfolds and have to think what might have happened to my team if they had kept their faith in him and not suffered that 44 day debacle."

It started at Anfield...

It all began at Anfield on Saturday, August 22, 1964. That day Liverpool played Arsenal, and that night highlights of the game were shown in the first-ever *Match of the Day*.

Today *Match of the Day* is very much part of our everyday lives. It's a national institution, as familiar as *Family Favourites* on the radio each Sunday or, as far as the youngsters are concerned, *Top of the Pops* on a Thursday evening.

But in the early days of the programme everything was very different. First of all it was shown on BBC2 and it attracted an audience of only about twenty thousand viewers. The screening time was different too. The programme began at 6.30 p.m. and at the time it was claimed that *Match of the Day* provided "an arrangement which gives football viewers who have been to their own matches in the afternoon an opportunity to get home and see the televised game."

And those early programmes were watched by even fewer than had actually attended League club grounds during the afternoon. By May 1966 the audience had risen to the million mark and at the start of the next season, with all England still embroiled in a football fervour as a result of that summer's magnificent World Cup victory, *Match of the Day* switched to BBC1.

There, of course, it has remained, going from strength to strength, its audience increasing out of all recognition until nowadays the programme's regular viewers are large enough in number to fill Wembley Stadium over 120 times!

The move over to BBC1 came as a result of new arrangements requested by the football authorities whereby the amount of football available to television should be reduced. The new deal meant that the BBC was entitled to screen its weekend soccer on Saturday evenings but not on Sunday afternoons, as had been the case with F.A. Cup matches the previous season. With the amount of football screened each week restricted, the BBC was determined to reach as wide an audience as possible with what *was* shown, hence the move to BBC1.

The channel switch coincided with the start of another long-running series, *Midnight Movie*. The first film screened in that series was *The Man Who Never Was*, so Clifton Webb and a line-up of famous British actors had a tenuous link with the first footballers to appear on *Match of the Day* on its new channel on that August 20.

In 1967, when the 100th edition was reached, the audience had grown to 7½ millions. Up until that date—Saturday, November 4—fifty Football League clubs had appeared on

the programme. Today there can only be a handful of teams who have not been featured.

With the F.A. Cup Final being televised in colour on BBC2 for the very first time in 1968, it was time for a League game to get the same treatment and so, in the following season, *Match of the Day*

Today there are only 16 clubs currently in the Football League who have not been visited by Match of the Day. Here are the cameras at Watford.

switched to BBC2 for one week only so that the first League game to be screened in colour could be transmitted. At this time, of course, BBC1 was still in black and white.

A New-Look Programme

A new-look *Match of the Day* was launched to coincide with the start of the new Football League season on Saturday, August 9, 1969. By now the audience had grown to a regular ten million, and with the new format the programme's running time was increased from 45 to 60 minutes.

Introduced by David Coleman, the programme made the undisputed claim that it was

"television's most comprehensive football programme." It featured one main, nationally screened match, plus highlights of a match involving a local team, to each of six regions: the Midlands, West, Wales, South East, North and Northern Ireland.

Commentators David Coleman and Kenneth Wolstenholme were joined by Barry Davies, who had switched channels from ITV; Wally Barnes, the former Arsenal and Wales skipper; and Idwal Robling.

A competition to find the best soccer crowd choir in Britain, organised by the Football League, was also a feature of that season's programmes.

In the first of the regionalised programmes the main match was between Crystal Palace and Manchester United. In the Midlands viewers also saw highlights of the Wolves versus Stoke City game; in the South East and North it was Leeds United versus Spurs; in the South and West, Southampton against West Bromwich Albion, and in Wales the local match was Wrexham against Exeter City.

Tighter and Slicker

By the start of the 1970/71 season it had been decided to make *Match of the Day* a tighter, slicker production by concentrating on the action from two of the most attractive fixtures of that day. The commentators were David Coleman, who also introduced the programme, Barry Davies, Alan Weeks and Kenneth Wolstenholme. Ex-schoolteacher Bob Wilson began an expert analysis spot, hurrying to the studio from his Saturday afternoon job of keeping goal for Arsenal! Today, of course, he is recognised as one of the most accomplished of television's soccer men and presents his own programme, *Football Focus*, each week in *Grandstand*.

Goal of the Month

The first 'Goal of the Month' competition was introduced in September 1970, and since then it has become established as a firm *Match of the Day* favourite. The number of voting postcards received from viewers continues to amaze, and delight, the production team, but since most football fans relish the sight of the ball hitting the back of the net—assuming it's not their own team's—it is perhaps easy to understand the competition's great attraction. The 'Goal of the Season' is, of course, a natural extension of the idea.

Popular Format

The work of improving and adjusting *Match of the Day* goes on unceasingly, but the basic format of the programme which has evolved over the years has remained basically unchanged for some time now. Each week highlights from two of the day's top League matches are featured, and for some rounds of the F.A. Cup the agreement with the football authorities means that three games can be covered. Topical soccer matters are discussed and the games seen are analysed in an informative way.

It is all rounded off with a look at the rest of the day's results and a look at the current League tables. *Match of the Day* lives up to that claim of the 1960s that it is 'television's most comprehensive football programme'.

The voice that kick d off...
Kenneth Wolstenholme

One man's name is synonymous with *Match of the Day*—the show's first commentator, Ken Wolstenholme.

He's reported on more matches than anyone else, having been behind the mike from the kick-off.

Today Ken's no longer connected with the programme and instead works for ITV's Tyne Tees Television—mainly reporting on matches in the North East, but in those early days he was very much the man around whom the show revolved.

He came out of the Royal Air Force in 1949 (after being decorated for bravery) and was working for BBC Radio in Manchester when he wrote to the Outside Broadcast Department in London suggesting that he would make a good television commentator.

In those days television was confined to London and when he journeyed to the capital for an audition Ken had not even seen television, let alone worked in it.

His audition was covering an amateur match at Romford, and some weeks later he was invited to return to the Essex ground to commentate on another amateur game between representative sides from the North and the South.

In that first match he shared the duties with Jimmy Jewell, a former referee who had given the penalty that decided the 1937–38 F.A. Cup Final.

When Jimmy died after a heart attack Ken was left as BBC TV's only soccer commentator and from covering the occasional big match became reg larly employed in that role when firstly *Today's Sport* and then *Sports Special* were launched as forerunners to *Match of the Day*.

Ken has lost count of the matches he has covered throughout the world but here recalls some of the personalities he met as *Match of the Day* commentator.

Ken Wolstenholme as *Match of the Day* viewers knew him.

BILL SHANKLY: Came into his own when you interviewed him. Absolutely tremendous for television. Even if his team had been heavily beaten he would come out with a tremendous quote, such as, "We outplayed them—and they had four breakaways and scored each time." He would say it so seriously!

DON REVIE: Good—but dour.

HARRY HASLAM: Could give up football and go on the halls as a comic.

BRIAN CLOUGH: A tremendous man to interview.

LAWRIE McMENEMY: Ask him a question and he'll answer it.

DANNY BLANCHFLOWER: He would talk his head off. You only had to ask him one question and he would take over the rest of the interview. So articulate and such a deep thinker that he was a must for after-the-match interviews.

DEREK DOUGAN: We discovered that during the match Derek would always know where the cameras were and would always go and wave in front of them. He was also the first out of the bath, dressed and with his hair right in case we wanted to talk to someone.

RODNEY MARSH: Just made for television. The only time we ever did the League Cup Final he scored a marvellous goal for Queen's Park Rangers.

GEORGE BEST: Again a fabulous personality for television—but he was always too shy to be interviewed.

BOBBY CHARLTON: Another man who was always hard going to interview. He hated that part of life although he was—and still is—a wonderful person.

NOBBY STILES: Tremendous character who appealed to the mums. We used to get letters from them saying it was terrible the way this little fellow was being treated by other players. All the mums jumped to his defence even though he was one of the toughest players in the game. He never bothered about anything—and never worried about putting his teeth back in for interviews.

DENIS LAW: Another who hated being interviewed. I'm surprised he's done so well as a radio summariser as he never wanted to talk about himself as a player. He used to ask for an outrageous fee—not because he wanted the money but because he thought it would stop

KEN BROWN: A great jovial character with West Ham. He anyone asking him to appear in front of the cameras.

only scored one goal in his career—and we had it.

PAT JENNINGS: He gave me my biggest problem as a commentator in a Charity Shield game at Wembley. The ball was passed back to him from outside the penalty area, and he picked it up and kicked it high. It caught the wind and bounced over Alex Stepney's head in the Manchester United goal. I thought 'it can't be a goal' then I thought 'but why not?' I don't think any of the players realised it was a goal because it was such an extraordinary happening.

GEOFF HURST: Another great personality because he did what the viewers wanted to see—score goals.

MARTIN PETERS: A tremendous footballer but on television his work is overlooked. He was so vital to West Ham during their glory days but it was always Hurst who looked the better player.

JIMMY GREAVES: Probably scored more *Match of the Day* goals than anyone else. I still remember one goal against Manchester United when he tip-toed through everyone to score.

PETER OSGOOD: Provided one of the programme's red-faced moments in a game against Liverpool. He made a fantastic run which was so out of this world that it took everyone's breath away and had the Kop giving him an ovation. On the way back to London on the train the producer Alec Weekes and myself were raving about this bit of magic. We got to the studio to watch the edited version and it wasn't in. Someone had cut it out and when asked why had replied: "He didn't score—did he?" It was one of those things that can happen—but doesn't happen anywhere near as often as everyone fears.

Covering a West Ham–Sheffield United *Match of the Day* **on February 19th 1966, in the early days of the programme. Notice the BBC2 camera and the gloves to keep him warm in the commentary box.**

In Focus 🄲 Martin Peters

In Focus ⚽ Stan Bowles

In Focus ⚽ Paul Mariner

My Role
Jimmy Hill

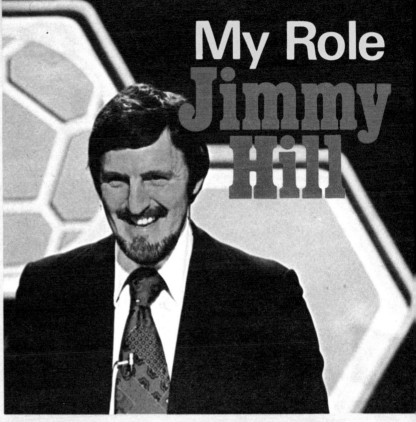

Jimmy Hill is a man of many parts. Television pundit, soccer professor, fund-raising golfer, Sunday newspaper journalist, and stock-breeder.

He is also the man the referees call Clinical Jimmy—with an audience of millions every Saturday night.

His is a complex life in which he has business interests spread as far afield as the oil sheikdoms of the Middle East and the two car-worker dominated areas of Coventry, England, and Detroit, America.

Let's take a look at the lifestyle of Hill, the ex-pro whose playing career was ended with a knee injury and whose midfield scheming was confined mainly to Fulham.

He now runs soccer in Saudi Arabia through the World Sports Academy, and flies to the oil-rich states at least once a month.

His contract—won in the face of competition from West Germany, Brazil and other powerful footballing nations—is with the Government, and Hill likens the exercise to running a University—with soccer the only subject.

He says: "The first thing we have to do is to get our players to the standard of our neighbours Iran and Kuwait. Then the next objective must be to get into the World Cup Finals.

"Quite honestly my role is really only advisory because we have people to do all the jobs that need doing. It's planning for the future. Already the players have improved but what happens depends on the amount of coaching and the creation of facilities. Those are the twin aims of the Government—they have the talent to win through."

Hill's standing in the soccer world was underlined when his consortium successfully bid for the franchise to start soccer in Detroit.

He's now termed an owner of Detroit Express and one of his first jobs was to gather together a team to open the American season.

"It was satisfying to win that franchise against the sort of opposition we faced in Saudi," Hill revealed.

His third soccer administrative post is at Highfield Road, Coventry—the setting for one of his greatest triumphs when his own brand of salesmanship turned a creaking club into one of the most forward-seeking and prosperous in the land.

His first involvement in soccer management was at the Midlands club where he changed the team colours and latched onto a local journalist's description of his team as the Sky Blues to launch a football revolution.

He not only took Coventry to the First Division but turned the club into Super-League fan status with his off-the-park promotions that persuaded the big-earning car workers at Jaguar and British Leyland to spend their Saturday afternoons watching soccer.

Little wonder then that he was invited back as the club's managing director. He spends at least one day a week at the club and serves as a sounding board for any ideas or thoughts from manager Gordon Milne.

"I leave the manager to run the team but usually if he wants to buy or sell a player he'll come to me and we'll talk about it together. That's one of the departments that comes into my brief."

Jimmy Hill Limited also act as advisors to the London based Sportsman Club and once a month Jimmy takes over the organisation of their Sportsman of the Month Award night.

Outside his own widespread business interests the bearded Hill is also deeply involved in charity work.

He's chairman of Goaldiggers—an organization that is linked with the National Playing Fields Association and which raises money to provide hard area soccer pitches in under-privileged areas.

Three other charities which demand his time are the Variety Club Golfing Society—in a year they raised more than £100,000; SPARKS, a sports-dominated charity that aids research into crippling diseases by way of celebrity events, including motor-races at Brands Hatch; and Riding for the Disabled.

At one time he was also a member of the Sports Council but resigned his seat after a lengthy spell of service so that he could concentrate more time on his pet charities.

Additionally he provides post-match comments for the *News of the World* and has been compiling a new book on the One Hundred Best Footballers.

How, then, did this ex-Stock Exchange clerk become such a powerful figure in Britain's sports hierarchy?

Hill recounts his early days: "I started coaching as soon as I went to play for Brentford. I went to Lilleshall because I was interested in learning. I started going to coach at schools, and then at Oxford and London Universities. I then became chairman of the Professional Footballers' Association for five years, and that gave me the confidence to speak in public."

It was during that spell that Hill launched his brilliant campaign to re-write the soccer player's contract and that, more than anything else, brought him into the public eye.

Continued Hill: "Then my knee happened and I had to give up football. I had always insisted that the chairman of the P.F.A. should be a current player. Before me it had been a paid chairman. I was the first player to become chairman and obviously had to give it up when I retired.

"I spent two or three months trying to work out what I would do when I was offered the job as manager of Coventry City. We needed people in the ground because we needed to make money. I found I was only coaching the team for two hours a day so there was other time available to do other things at the club. I identified the need to get more people interested in Coventry and started to think of ways to do it.

"Earlier I had written a book —Striking Soccer—which was meant to be a plea for the cause but which turned out to be a record of what went on in the players' battle for freedom. In that I had talked about the need to think about the game's future.

"One of the first things I did at Coventry was to redesign the shirts to get a modern, different style. I wanted a smart design to give the players more pride in themselves.

"A local journalist nicknamed us the Sky Blues and we latched onto it and used it in our favour. You can't have all the good ideas yourself and you have got to be prepared to use someone else's idea to your own advantage."

Hill was also expanding into the field of communications during his reign as Coventry's manager. As chairman of the P.F.A. he had presented a fine image on television and in 1966 the BBC invited him to work for them at the World Cup.

He takes up the story of his entry into a full-time television career: "I left Coventry at the end of 1967—the year we got up to the First Division. People said I left to join London Weekend Television but that wasn't true. I had already left before I had an offer to go there as Head of Sport.

"I was an executive seven days a week doing programmes at the weekend and office work five days a week. I could only go on so long doing that and when my contract came to an end the BBC offered me a job as a performer only and I started Jimmy Hill Limited. I've been at the BBC ever since. Originally it was intended that I would only analyse matches but then I was asked to front the programme. I was worried, but now I enjoy it."

What does Hill, a qualified referee, see as his role on *Match of the Day*? A crusading campaigner to cure the game's ills? A sole arbiter on dubious decisions?

"People think *Match of the Day* should fight causes," he says, "but we have done that. One idea I tried to get referees to adopt was a system of making sure the goalkeeper did not move at a penalty. They should look at the goalkeeper—and be listening for the thud when the boot hits the ball. That's the only way to make sure the goalkeeper doesn't move. Some referees say it doesn't work. All I know is that we tested it—and I know it's the nearest we could ever get to solve a problem.

"I like to look for the good things but all football's not like that. One week in four or five there's got to be bad things.

"We wouldn't examine a penalty if the result was 4-1. We wouldn't need to establish the truth then. Where there's argument and misunderstanding and disagreements we will go over the point to discover, as near as possible, the truth. My role is not to be unkind but if referees continually make mistakes or players continually play in a violent way we should be establishing the truth. Sometimes even with slow motion and my background of football we can't always get right at the truth—but that should always be our aim ... to tell the truth!"

In Focus Kenny Dalglish

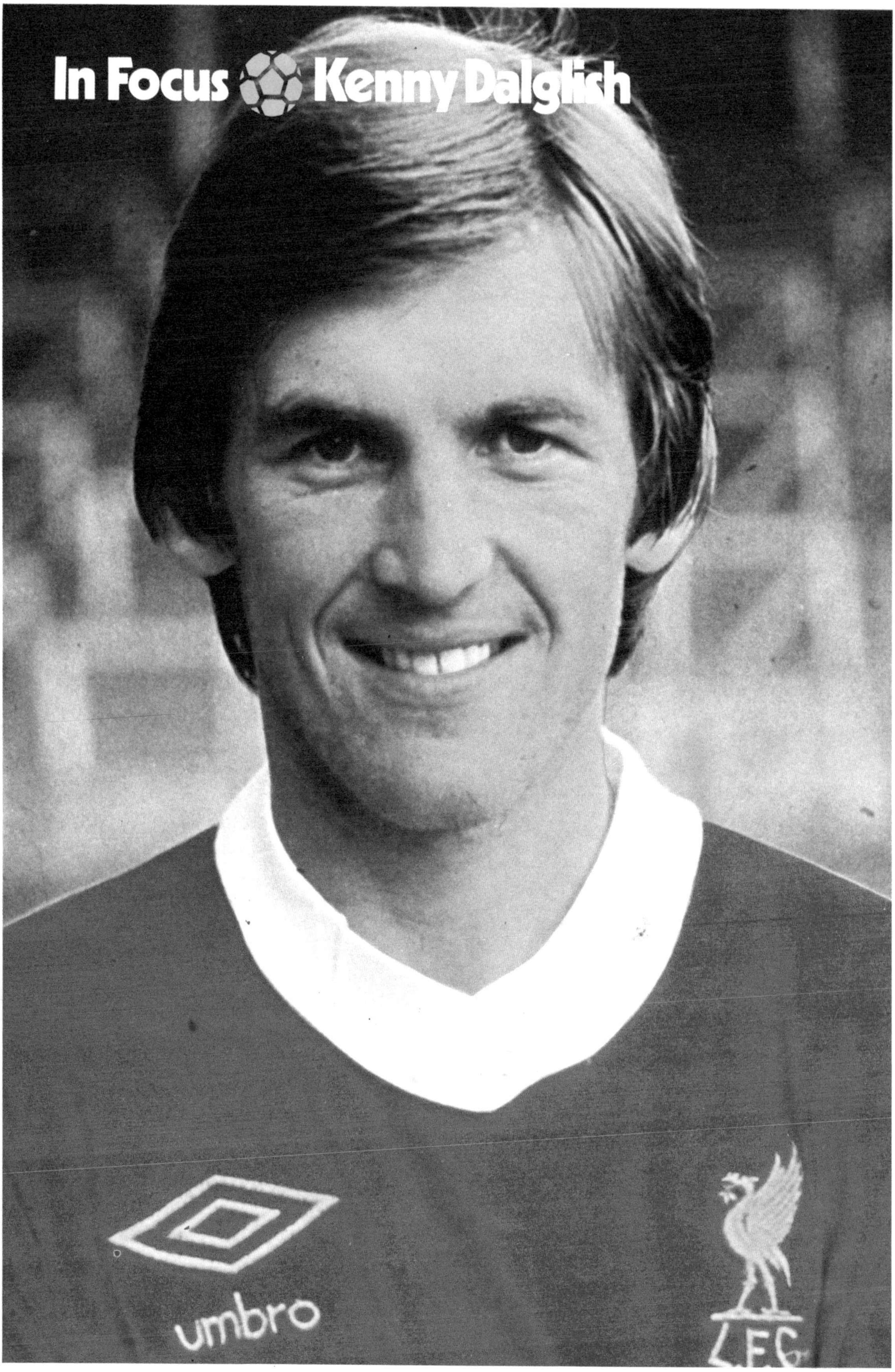

In Focus ⚽ **Sandy Jardine**

There's a goal on his birthday!

by Barry Davies

The image of a *Match of the Day* commentator is that of a globe-trotting traveller who swaps verbal punches with star players and managers—someone who arrives at a match a few hours before the kick-off, and whose job ends within a few minutes of the final whistle.

It's a job that anyone could do—at least if you believe the wags on the terraces.

But in reality it entails a lot more than is seen and heard every Saturday night.

Every hour of commentary can mean a day of detailed research before the event.

Most commentators have their own filing method and few conflict violently with the private system adopted by Barry Davies, the ex-medical student who was in ITV's 1966 World Cup team before joining the BBC.

"There are certain basic things which I try to keep up. I have a card index on all the players in the First Division and some in the Second Division.

"I have a newspaper cutting book on each season which goes back eight or nine seasons. And I keep a results sequence," explains Barry.

These records—and a near photographic memory—serve as the homework before every match. Sometimes, if he is covering a match from the lower leagues, Barry has to carry out thorough research, but on four Saturdays out of five he will be covering a game involving sides well documented in the Davies File.

A few days before the match he sits down— and begins the painstaking research that may not even be used when the game kicks off.

Barry explains his research routine.

"I will get out the results sequences of the two teams and will go over their results this season, their scorers, their running league position, the crowds and the full teams.

"I try to keep it up-to-date myself but if I am not completely accurate I'll give Jack Rollin a ring. He's a freelance journalist who keeps a mountain of facts and figures.

"I can pick up quite a lot from looking at the results sequences and find out how many matches each player has played in.

"I will either have a list of each team, or the squads from which the teams are chosen. Once I have that I'll bring out the player cards that I keep up-dated and go through them—picking out little points that will come in handy.

"Then if I need to check anything I can always go back through the cuttings books.

"The player card usually tells me a player's date of birth, his early career, his various debuts in league and international matches, his transfers, his total number of appearances and goals for clubs and any other special notes.

"I have a fairly comprehensive list of birth-dates although there are some clubs that will not divulge this information. I think it is important to have this, viewers like to know if a player is celebrating his birthday.

"If a new player comes into the team I might make inquiries about him on the Friday— perhaps have a chat to him myself.

"We also have two liaison officers on the programme who nip into the dressing rooms before a game and they will always ask if there is anything in particular I want to know.

"If I've not seen the two teams before I'll usually ask the clubs to send me copies of their last two home programmes—they can often give me a lot of information.

"One of our problems is that we are not like the local newspaperman who sees his own club every week and knows everything about them. We could go three months before seeing the same club so we have to rely on our home-work. The cuttings book is always kept up to date. I'll take clippings from Sunday papers, magazines or local papers. In fact I'll keep

anything I think might be useful in the future.

"I know that John Motson makes a habit of going to see the managers on the Friday before a match. I prefer not to do that. Instead I'll try and see them earlier in the week. It's a personal preference.

"Once I've done all that I make notes to take with me to the match. They are probably illegible to anyone but me.

"They will be general notes on players' appearances and goals. Perhaps a player hasn't scored for a long time—so I'll try to find out when he last scored just in case he gets on the scoresheet again so I can say that it is two years since he scored—and that was at Highbury against Arsenal.

"I'll also make a note of anything that might relate to the match I'm covering—perhaps it is three years ago that a player signed for his club; maybe he celebrated his birthday earlier in the week; or could have made his debut against that afternoon's opponents.

"Normally I'll read through the notes before a match and not refer to them during the game. Facts should come to you automatically while you are doing the commentary and you should not be trying to force your facts onto the viewer—the background should be just that rather than trying to make the circumstances fit the background."

SOCCER

One of the most popular programmes on television is *The Superstars*, the series in which top sportsmen from Britain and throughout Europe compete in various events. There's sprinting, swimming, shooting, weightlifting, gymnastic tests, rowing or canoeing, cycling, penalty kicking, table tennis and steeple-chasing. Every competitor must take part in eight of the ten events, the only trouble is—he mustn't enter for his own specialised sport.

Footballers have undoubtedly been among the most entertaining sportsmen who have appeared in *The Superstars*, although, apart from Kevin Keegan, they have failed to make much impact on the distribution of the prize money.

However one or two points have emerged about footballers as a result of the series. One thing, they can certainly run fast!

In their first appearances in the programme both Malcolm Macdonald and Mike Channon saw off the opposition in their 100 metres races in superb style. The stage was then set for a meeting between the two to decide which was the unofficial *Superstars* sprint champion. And, on paper at least, they weren't going to have things all

to themselves, for lined up alongside the two England strikers was the man reputed to be the fastest in Rugby Union—Gerald Davies.

But Supermac and Mike left the fleet-footed Welshman well behind as they sped down the straight with the burly Macdonald nosing in front at the line.

Kevin Keegan competes in the re-run of the cycle race. Note the bandage on his arm. The lacerations on his back cannot be seen from this angle.

Colin Bell takes the water jump in the steeple-chase in fine style.

Colin Bell confirmed his incredible stamina and demonstrated all too clearly why he got the nickname Nijinsky when he won the punishing steeple-chase with ease.

But the great memory all football fans must have of *The Superstars* must surely be the

So now we know who is the fastest! Mike Channon (left) and Malcolm Macdonald after their magnificent 100 metres battle.

SUPERSTARS

art-stopping exhibition of raw
urage and will to win of
vin Keegan.

He was still with Liverpool
en he took part in the pro-
amme, in a heat staged at
acknell in Berkshire. He
ived direct from playing in a
rity match on the continent.
the time he got there it was
l into the early hours of the
rning but at 8.00 a.m. sharp
was already in the swimming
l ready to collect his first
nts of the competition.

By the time the afternoon of
second, and last, day was
ched Kevin had victory in his

ter Shilton, who usually
ends his time making sure
t other people aren't on
get!

ght . . . all he had to do was
ck up a few points in the cycle
ce and score well in the
eeple-chase.

But his enthusiasm got the
tter of him and he came a
eadful cropper going into the
st bend of the cycle race. He
ashed heavily to the ground at
out thirty miles per hour,
verely bruising and cutting his
m and tearing most of the skin
f his shoulder as he scraped
ong the rough cinders.

Mike Channon enjoying his table tennis.

Malcolm Macdonald paddling his own canoe. Something his team mates certainly don't expect him to do!

Kevin Keegan, before his cycling accident, wearing his life jacket ready for the canoe race.

Medical assistance arrived
almost immediately but Kevin,
after a quick check-up and a
chance to steady himself, announced that he was going to
ignore the doctor's advice and
refused to go to hospital. "After
all," he said, "I've only got to
get into the cycling final and
then win the steeple-chase and
I've won the whole thing!"

And that is just what he did.

For more than twelve years, in fact ever since England won the World Cup in 1966, English football has been a wilderness for wingers.

Managers and coaches were quick to jump on the success band wagon that Sir Alf Ramsey had plotted for his successful England team and in no time at all the successful club teams seemed to be moulded from the same 'wingless wonders' pattern.

Things became so bad that wingers literally went out of fashion and were looked upon as old fashioned and out-of-date. Because of this attitude new young wingers ceased to emerge and fans had only memories of great wing play to look back on.

But recently tactics have been changing. Teams have again been more positive in their play and many are being successful as a result.

One of the 'old fashioned' wingers who has played consistently well during recent years is Everton's Dave Thomas. He's an out and out winger of the sort fans love to see taking on a full back in a race to get to the goal line to cross the ball.

Here's a fine action study of Dave Thomas against his previous club Queen's Park Rangers. The Londoners are in their change red and white strip to avoid a colour clash with the Merseysiders.

The Rangers' full back Dave Clement seems to have everything under control.

But Everton's persistent winger has other ideas.

Wingers are back

Dave Thomas wins the tussle for the ball and is quickly away.

He knocks the ball down the line and is already three yards clear in the race to the goal line. A classic piece of wing play.

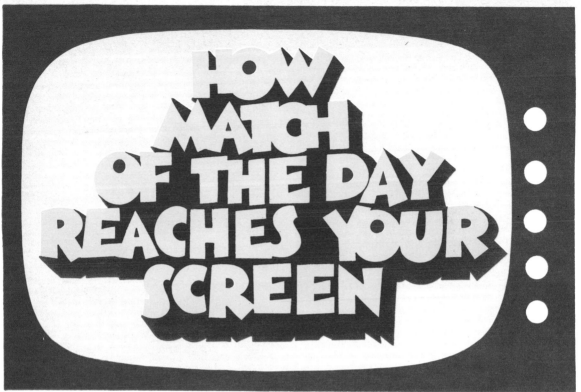

LIVE ... AT THE GROUND

Saturdays start early for Alec Weeks.

The Series Producer of *Match of the Day* is up and about at 7.00 a.m. "I must be up by 7 o'clock in case the weather is bad," says the man who worked on the very first *Match of the Day* in 1964 and who, in 1976, led the team whose coverage of the FA Cup Final was adjudged the best Outside Broadcast of the Year.

"The weather is a vital factor for us," explains Alec. "If a game is off for any reason I need to know as soon as possible so that we can put contingency plans for covering an alternative match into operation. I keep in close touch with clubs all over England during periods of bad weather.

"There are occasions when I reckon I know more about the weather conditions and prospects throughout the country than any meteorologist. If, when I wake up, the weather is bad then I get down to the ground where the game is coming from by 7.30 a.m., and if I believe the match is in real jeopardy then I get on the telephone fast. I can't wait for the referee to arrive, usually at about 9 o'clock. By then we'd have wasted valuable time."

But today, thankfully the game is not in danger and Alec has time to study the team lists he always has beside his hotel bed: "It helps make the names stick in my mind," he believes. After breakfast he telephones Editor Jonathan Martin at home at 8.30 a.m. to confirm that all is well. He leaves the hotel with his assistant Julie and gets to the ground at 9.30 a.m. He goes straight up on the gantry to the main camera positions. The cameramen are not yet at the ground and Alec talks to the riggers, the men who erect the television equipment, and the senior engineer. At the same time his eyes scan probingly around the stadium, checking everything in sight.

Between 9.30 and 10.00 a.m. the cameramen arrive and the talk is about football and the afternoon's game: "I know he's not Bobby Charlton or Gordon Hill," says Alec, referring to one of the visiting players, "but he can still hit them from outside the box. Don't get sucked in too tight. If you do the ball will be in the net and we'll miss it. Remember, not too much of a close-up on any player who is liable to shoot from a long way out."

The cameramen all have their say and Alec encourages them to do so: "This is essentially a team job we do. The cameramen, the commentator and myself all follow each other if we're doing the job properly. Throughout a match we take it in turns to lead and everyone else, because of our training, follows the man who has picked up a particular aspect of play.

At 11.00 a.m. it's time to drop in and see the home club's secretary: "I know most of them well, but none of us have much time to spare on match days so after the usual pleasantries I collect the 15 match programmes we need for the production team and then head for the mobile control room, or scanner as we call it, to prepare for the rehearsal."

The rehearsal continues from just after 11.00 a.m. until 12.30 p.m. During it the whole production team concentrate on discipline. "Discipline," according to Alec, "is the key to televising football. Each cameraman knows what shots to look for and from what angle he is to cover the match.

"One camera covers the game in wide angle, seeing the forward line sweep up, the defence fall back. Another goes for the close-up shots of solo dribbles or vicious tackles and another looks for the personality pictures of individual players. The fourth camera meanwhile concentrates on crowd scenes, incidents off the pitch, etc. If a penalty is awarded I haven't time to tell one camera to go to the man who has been fouled, another to pick up the victim, another the referee and another to see what's happening on the trainers' bench.

"They must all provide the correct pictures instantly! Then I can let viewers at home see separate shots of everyone involved all within about ten seconds."

The outside broadcast unit behind the stand means that Match of the Day is there.

During the rehearsal the team go through just about every conceivable incident likely to occur during the match. Corner kicks, throwins, free-kicks, penalties. All are rehearsed.

"O.K., so we've been doing this for the last thirty weeks or so," admits Alec, "but this is a different ground with different shots, different angles and therefore different problems. We must do everything possible to help our work. I try to tell the cameramen everything, do whatever they ask and help them in every way I can. Then if something goes wrong there can be no excuses."

Senior cameraman Alistair Mitchell talking to his colleagues Paul Harding and Martin Mathewson in the deserted stadium.

At 12.30 p.m. the television crew break for lunch and over the meal the conversation is, predictably, about football.

But soon it's back to work and at 1.30 p.m. LINE-UP begins. This means the engineers ensuring that the pictures from each of the cameras line up in every way with the pictures as they are received back in the Television Centre in London. All the details of the pictures, including the colours, must correspond exactly.

While this is going on Alec Weeks pops into the dressing room area to see the referee and meet the managers: "I don't have much to do with the players," he says. "I might get to like or dislike some, which perhaps could influence the way I cover incidents in which they are involved."

As the teams arrive, almost together at about 1.45 p.m., Alec is talking to Bill Platts, the production team's liaison man who during the course of the afternoon assists in numerous aspects of the operation: "Check we are sure of the team colours, Bill, and that the ref remembers to pick up the white ball. Oh yes, and don't forget to confirm with the ref that we can take the half-way line flag out, it's right in front of our touch-line camera."

If the camera low-down on the touch-line had been positioned in one half of the field, the referee would have been asked if he would be willing to arrange for his linesmen to avoid that part of the line and use the opposite side of the pitch.

At 2.15 p.m. it's 'off with his jacket and down to work' for Alec, as he settles in the scanner

Alec Weeks (centre) in the scanner. Engineering Manager John Kemp is nearest the camera.

before the array of monitor screens. Next he opens his first packet of chewing gum and asks for the live pictures of *Grandstand* which are being shown to be turned off: "From now on there's no more chit chat," he advises everyone. "Business begins."

The talk-back, the sound communication between the cameramen and all other vital production people, is a babel of voices, but there is no surplus noise in the scanner. No cheering or displays of emotion or frustration are allowed.

"There's enough talk that's vital," barks Alec.

This is surely true. Sitting within feet of each other and talking urgently into their tiny microphones are the Engineering Manager, whose job it is to co-ordinate all the technicalities and in effect make the whole operation work; Julie, the Producer's Assistant, who is constantly talking to Jonathan Martin and the video tape recording engineers in London as well as sorting out a hundred and one problems of varying urgency, and Alec Weeks himself who, of course, has to talk almost non-stop throughout. On top of all this, coming in from elsewhere are numerous other voices, some intermittently but others, like the commentator's, incessantly.

It's almost 3.00 p.m. and kick-off is any moment. News and information keep filtering through to the scanner and the commentator from Bill Platts, who is constantly on the move. In the players' tunnel, the dressing rooms, popping up in the Press Box, talking to people in corridors—Bill is the man who keeps the *Match of the Day* team and, in due course, the viewers at home, aware of the very latest developments.

If a player is unexpectedly left out of a match, Bill discovers why. If during a game there is confusion about which player has scored a goal, then Bill checks with the team bench. Maybe a surprise substitution will be made. If so, Bill will establish if it was for tactical reasons or due to injury.

The 45 minutes from the kick-off to half-time flash by. The scanner is noisy but every word spoken has a purpose. Alec Weeks is like a ring master. His concentration is total, as his eyes dart about the bank of screens before him, his fingers hovering over the buttons with which he is able to select for screening any of the pictures before him.

The scanner is the heart of the operation and Weeks controls its beat. He talks constantly to the cameramen. Sometimes he bullies them, sometimes he cajoles, sometimes he even persuades . . . anything to achieve the best results.

"Watch their eyes," he says as a cameraman searches for which defender/attacker pair of opponents are vying for a high ball cleared from defence. In the confines of his viewfinder the cameraman cannot see the ball, just the players he is focused upon. He must judge correctly. If the ball goes instead to another pair of players then viewers at home will wonder what is happening.

Suddenly it's half-time and the tension relaxes.

"Unwind everyone," says Alec. "I'd love a cup of tea." He stretches and looks around optimistically, at the same time asking Julie to get the Television Centre on the line. Within seconds he is talking to Jonathan Martin about the events of the first half.

His tea arrives as the teams are about to come out again. He gulps it down, checks that all departments—cameramen, commentator, sound, engineering, etc.—are O.K. and ready to go. Then it's on with the game.

As in the first 45 minutes the pace is fast and furious: "The cameramen are really trying," says Alec, "and you can't ask for more than that. We don't want just good cameramen, they must be brilliant!"

The second half seems to be over even more quickly than the first, but even when the final whistle goes there is still plenty to be done and the production team are still on their toes.

Alec has a rapid conversation with Jonathan Martin and relays to Bill Platts the names of the players wanted for interviews that may be included in the programme. While these players are being asked to hurry their baths and make their way to the camera, the commentator is doing his match report live into *Grandstand*. This time there is no interview needed for the end of *Grandstand* and so mercifully the time factor is not perhaps quite as acute as it is sometimes.

The match report is completed smoothly and without fuss, and suddenly there's only the *Match of the Day* interview left to do. It has been decided that the manager of the winning team will be interviewed together with a player from the opposition. All goes well and at exactly 5.30 p.m. it is all over and the business of packing up begins.

For Alec Weeks and his team the air of anti-climax is inescapable. Post-mortems are already in progress as Alec talks to as many of the crew as he can. He and the cameramen could talk about what happened and how they should have covered it for hours. But everyone is tired. It's been a long day and Alec must pop into the Board Room to see the managers, secretary and chairmen.

"I always like to get to the Board Room pretty quickly," he smiles. "A cup of tea is the priority after the game and that's one place I know we can all get one.

"The tea service varies from club to club. They're all good really, but at Arsenal they're exceptional. There they have a silver tea pot specially reserved for the *Match of the Day* team!"

At 6.30 p.m. Alec, Julie and most of the BBC personnel leave the club and set out for the station to catch the train back to London. None of them enjoy the travelling particularly but, as Alec himself put it: "As long as we can get home to watch television by about 10.00 p.m. tonight it isn't too bad!"

It's 2.40 p.m. as Jimmy Hill, bearded and denimed, walks into the main reception area at BBC Television Centre. He takes the lift to the second floor and purposefully strides into Room 2142 where the legend on the door reads: International Commentary Suite. There he is greeted by *Match of the Day* editor Jonathan Martin, studio director John Rowlinson, producer Mike Murphy and London University soccer coach Jim Clarkson, a studious, quiet man whose afternoon duties

will be to log every shot, save, foul and incident.

It's one of the most important afternoons of the entire season. F.A. Cup sixth round day—three hours from Wembley. This time ITV have won the toss for choice of games and left the BBC covering the tantalising West Bromwich Albion v Nottingham Forest and Orient v Ipswich ties while ITV have their cameras focused on Wrexham-Arsenal and Middlesbrough-Orient—obviously gambling on at least one major upset.

For nearly three-quarters of an hour the two monitors bringing in pictures from the Hawthorns and The Den have been jerking into spontaneous action. A third screen shows the live *Grandstand* programme and a smaller colour set perched above shows the shots from an isolator camera at The Den. It is this camera that will bring the action replay from behind the goal. A cowboy style shoot-out provides pre-match entertaining at Millwall and the order goes out: "Get a shot of the coffin for us will you—it might do for a closing shot of somebody's cup hopes."

It's never used. The afternoon ahead is to provide enough of its own headlines without fear of having to resort to gimmicks.

Occasionally the voices of commentators John Motson and Barry Davies crackle over the lines as they rehearse their opening introduction or seek last-minute advice on technical coverage.

Down in VT Recording Area One—two floors underground—teams of technicians are recording both matches on giant oversize home movie outfits.

They record everything that's punched out by the on-the-spot director and it is here that the split-timing job of editing ninety minutes of action into less than a third of that will take place later in the evening. Each half is recorded on a spool. And it is also down here in the basement that the Beeb's only video tape disc is situated. It's not used during the actual match itself as first priority on its Saturday afternoon services goes to the live *Grandstand*.

Kick-off—and everyone settles down. Talking stops except for the odd interjection by statistician Jim Clarkson; a cry of 'handball' from pipe-smoking Jimmy Hill; or an order from Jonathan Martin.

After ten minutes Ipswich go ahead—and a direct link from Room 2142 to the *Grandstand* studios more than a mile away in Lime Grove allows presenter Frank Bough to bring the news to viewers within a minute of the ball hitting the back of the net.

It's a situation that is to be repeated time after time on this controversial afternoon. The all-First Division clash is warming up and West Brom go ahead. Minutes later a close-up camera shot shows Ally Brown asking himself 'How did I miss that?' after another close shave for Brian Clough's treble-chasers.

"Did you see that?" asks Hill. "He didn't swear—most of them would have done."

Albion continue to push forward on the right-hand monitor while on the opposite flank play is being held up at Millwall because

Ally Brown, W.B.A.

of a disturbance behind one of the goals.

Grandstand ask for a live report on the situation from John Motson who is, initially, warned not to talk of a pitch invasion as the first shots suggest fans being deliberately brought onto the park because of congestion. Later the words 'pitch invasion' have more relevance as Ipswich manager Bobby Robson is to present *Match of the Day* with a tricky problem.

Eighteen minutes' play are to be lost in South London because of the crowd trouble—and 120 miles away Forest are to lose their dreams of the treble.

Cyrille Regis scores West Brom's second as the first half of the other match comes to a delayed finish.

Paul Mariner hits Ipswich's second as Nottingham Forest launch a real counter-offensive. Jonathan Martin makes his major decision at 4.25 p.m.—and informs everyone: Unless there's a startling turn around at Millwall, West Brom-Nottingham Forest will be the main match. Close-up of a smiling Ron Atkinson: "That'll make a nice shot for the titles at the end of the show."

Mariner puts Ipswich three-up and a voice in the Viewing Room opines "It's a bore now." He spoke too soon. A dramatic finale makes it 6-1 for the Division One side and this late goal flurry persuades the editor to readjust his timing of the two matches.

Originally the end of Clough's dream was to be given five minutes more than the action from Cold Blow Lane. The Ipswich rampage forces him to split the 45 minutes of allowed action into segments of 23 minutes and 22 minutes with the WBA-Forest clash still leading off the show.

Jonathan Martin and Jimmy Hill.

Games are over. The work continues. John Motson scurries off to find Bobby Robson for an interview—'nothing long, just about a minute'—while Barry Davies has to seek out West Brom manager Ron Atkinson and someone from the depressed Forest camp. Archie Gemmill agrees and both interviews are to be shown later.

While the respective crews are polishing off their afternoon's work Jimmy Hill leaves to telephone his *News of the World* comment piece and shortly after 5.30 p.m. the interviews have been recorded.

The party—now shorn of Jim Clarkson, who has done his duty and produced statistics which showed that West Brom's two goals came with their first shots of each half—retires to an adjoining conference room, where facilities are shared with several shows including *Panorama* and *The Money Programme*.

For nearly two hours the production team discuss that evening's programme. Decisions are made as to which pieces of action will be needed to illustrate Jimmy Hill's analysis.

The format of that evening's show is

dissected. Someone suggests that they should try and speak to Orient manager Jimmy Bloomfield from his bed in the London Clinic where he has had an open line to Ayresome Park throughout the afternoon.

Medical permission to speak to Jimmy is sought—and received. Checks are made on the latest situation regarding the Millwall crowd violence. 'What will the News show of the crowd scenes?'

Lunch boxes (a scotch egg, a tomato, a couple of rolls, a meringue, a Mars bar and a bottle of orangeade) are brought in as there will be no time for even a canteen meal until the closing strains of the *Match of the Day* theme music bring an end to another day.

Jimmy Hill says he wants to emphasise the part that referee Pat Partridge played in the major tie. Others ask: 'Tell the viewers why Forest lost, Jim. Where did it all go wrong for them?'

Slowly the show is pieced together and each script is timed to make sure the show doesn't over-run its scheduled 59 minutes 30 seconds.

At 7.25 p.m. Jimmy Hill leaves—to retire to the Kensington Hilton to change from his denim outfit to a sober grey suit.

Twenty minutes later the action switches to Videotape Recording Area One in South Hall. There the activity is frenzied as production assistants edit the full match into the demanded 23 or 22 minutes.

Allowances have to be made for insertion of action replays.

The £80,000 machine can slow down the action automatically to half or one-fifth normal speed; and manually right down to a frame at a time.

By eight o'clock it is obvious that there are problems fitting everything into the 59.30. Jonathan Martin asks for another minute and informs Scotland—who have their own Saturday evening show—that this request has been granted.

Jimmy Hill in make-up.

Jonathan Martin talks to Jimmy Hill.

John Motson, who has rushed back from Millwall to the Lime Grove Studios to prepare that evening's news bulletin, is told he has $2\frac{1}{2}$ minutes to cover the rest of the day's soccer and shortly afterward Barry Davies arrives at VTR, having travelled back from the Midlands by train.

At 8.45 p.m. the action switches to Lime Grove—Studio E—1.2 miles from the Television Centre. During the afternoon the studio has been occupied by *Grandstand*—now the backroom boys are setting up for *Match of the Day*.

Newsroom staff study reports and flashes from the tape machines and discover that Bobby Robson has advocated using flame-throwers against the thugs who disrupted the Millwall match.

Because of this Jimmy Hill has to amend his script. John Motson prepares his news bulletin. Then he rehearses and has to cut out 26 seconds because he's over-running.

It's now 9.45 p.m. and the pace is hotting up. Jimmy Hill also does a dry-run. Back at Television Centre the editing team is working against the clock to get finished in time.

Ten-nineteen: two minutes to transmission. One minute to transmission. Thirty seconds. Run VT. 9-8-7-6-5-4-3-2-1. . . . The opening titles appear and the pre-recorded introduction is beamed out to 16 million viewers while Jimmy Hill is rehearsing his analysis.

Debate rages as to the best way to cover Robson's outburst—should it be ignored? No, it can't be as it was on the news.

The first match ends. Now it's live from Studio E. Then the second match. Back to Jimmy Hill and John Motson. It's 11.20 p.m. and the closing titles are cued. There's that shot of a smiling Ron Atkinson.

Everyone breathes a sigh of relief. And seven minutes later most people are on their way home—to try and watch the Midnight Movie!

It began with

"Let's have something different."

"Can't we get a designer who doesn't know anything about football? Why not ask a girl to see what she can come up with?"

It was with these words that Martin Hopkins, then the studio producer of *Match of the Day*, set the creative ball rolling that eventually resulted in the unique opening title sequence which heralds the start of each programme.

He was speaking to John Aston of BBC Television's Graphics Design Department about the series of *Match of the Day* which was to begin within the next few weeks.

And that is how Pauline Talbot came into the picture. She takes up the story: "When I was told that I was to work on the new titles for *Match of the Day* I nearly fell off my stool. I watch football, mainly on television, but I'm certainly no expert.

"I went away to think about it. For me, as a strictly casual observer, one of the great features of any soccer match is the crowd. It's the spectators who provide the atmosphere and excitement. The magic comes as a result of a large number of people reacting as a

Jimmy Hill looks alright . . . it's just a matter of sorting the sides out now!

single unit. People are very gregarious and this instinct is a dominant feature of a match. I love the atmosphere of a big crowd.

"Whenever I think of crowds I think of China and the magnificent rallies held there. As I considered ideas for *Match of the Day* I thought of a picture I had seen in a magazine years ago of 8,000 Chinese children holding up cards to form a picture of Chairman Mao. They call it card flashing.

"Anyway, this picture came to mind as I was wrestling with the problem of the new titles. I had to find a basic structure that would allow us to create an impact and

Youngsters in the 2,000 strong special 'crowd' are entertained with pop records while they wait for filming to start.

at the same time retain the football association that *Match of the Day* were anxious to keep.

"I felt that if I could base it on the Chairman Mao idea it would enable us to use the large crowd element I wanted and at the same time intersperse the quick bursts of football action."

There was one major problem to be overcome. How in Britain can you organise a vast group of people to act in complete unison in a disciplined manner? And even if such a group can be found, where can they be put so that they can be filmed?

Martin Hopkins recalls how that difficulty was solved: "We approached the Army and the police. Neither rated our idea as a practical proposition. Remember we needed 2,000 people to make it work. It wasn't hard to work out that we would have to use a stadium as the location, and that school children were the most likely subjects.

"The fresh problem was getting such a vast number to a suitable place. We scoured maps, looking for a stadium with two schools

Chairman Mao

very nearby. The children would have to be near enough to walk there. The prospect of trying to organise coaches for that sort of number was just too daunting!"

But there was such a stadium ... Queen's Park Rangers' ground at Loftus Road in West London.

"The fact that it was just around the corner from our studios was a complete coincidence," says Martin. "The Hammersmith County Girls' School and the Christopher Wren Boys' School are very near and we were delighted to receive magnificent help from the Inner London Education Authority and the head teachers and the staffs of both schools. Without their great support the entire venture would have definitely failed."

Many meetings later—between Martin Hopkins and Pauline Talbot on one side and the teachers and pupils on the other—the great day arrived. Pauline Talbot had used an enormous warehouse to produce the giant pictures which were then cut up into squares, one for each person in the huge montage. In all there were eight different pictures, each containing the two thousand separate cards. Every card was numbered and the exact location of each separate card and the number on the back was noted on a large sheet of graph paper.

"This was the only way we were

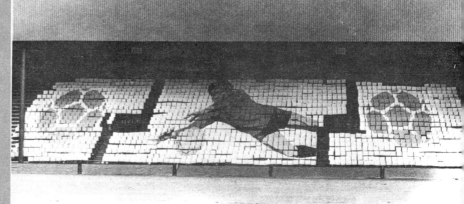

A perfect picture of a fine save.

able to talk to anyone in the crowd who wasn't holding their card correctly," explained Martin. "If a card representing, say the tip of Jimmy Hill's nose, was out of position, I was able to look on my graph, check the number at fault and call out that number through a microphone, asking if the person holding that card could please get it right."

The worst moment came for Martin Hopkins and Pauline Talbot seconds before the youngsters, and the thirty teachers who accompanied them, were asked to lift the cards for the first time.

Says Martin: "Nobody knew whether it would work or not. It could have been a complete disaster, but miraculously the picture appeared as if by magic. Then we knew we were really in business."

But it still wasn't that easy. If just one person gave in to the temptation to peer over the top of their card the effect would have been severely impaired. But the children realised the importance of getting it right so that all the filming could be completed on time.

"It was a great moment when I saw it work for the first time," recalls Martin. "I must admit, when Pauline first suggested the idea I thought she was off her head, but she was so persistent I found myself warming to the plan and getting more and more enthusiastic.

"There's not much doubt about it. They must be the biggest set of titles in television!"

The youngsters get it right again.

HANDS, KNEES

The *Match of the Day* cameramen pride themselves on their ability to recognise all the top players . . . even from a snapshot of their knees!

Before every F.A. Cup Final series producer Alec Weekes puts his top men through the knees test. He hands them a set of postcard photographs of players from both sides —and sends them away to study the photos, then he puts them through their paces, asking them to put a name to the knees.

Said Alec: "Nine times out of ten they are right. You've got to remember that the cameramen are usually down at pitch level and if I ask them to close in on a player they have to do it through their viewfinder. There isn't time to start searching for a player, so sometimes they may see a pair of knees— and have to know who that player is."

It's doubtful if anyone but an expert would be able to match the ace cameramen —but for fun why don't you test your skill at instant recognition?

To make it a little bit easier we've put faces and names to the knees—all you have to do is to link them up. It's not such a kneesy task, is it?

LOU MACARI

JIMMY CASE

DUNCAN McKENZIE

DENNIS MORTIMER

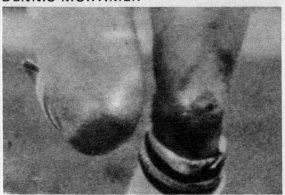

A

AND...

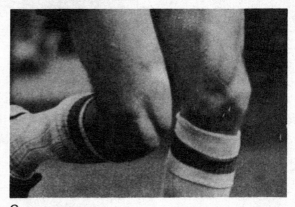

C

ALLAN CLARKE

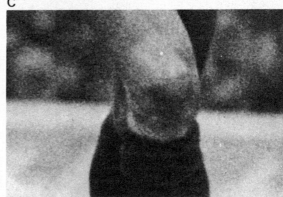

D

KEVIN KEEGAN

E

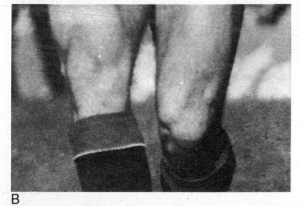

B

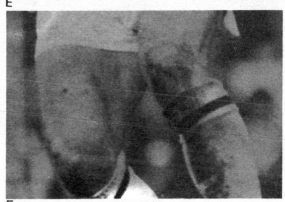

F

ANSWERS: Knees 1—Allan Clarke (E); Knees 2—Lou Macari (A); Knees 3—Kevin Keegan (F); Knees 4—Jimmy Case (B); Knees 5—Duncan Mckenzie (C); Knees 6—Dennis Mortimer (D).

55

My Cup Hero Mate
by John Motson

It was to be my first F.A. Cup tie. The two teams were non-league Hereford United and mighty Newcastle United, cup giants of the past. They had drawn 2-2 at Newcastle and, while everyone else was playing in the Fourth Round, they had their Third Round replay.

I probably got the match because it was the least important of the games Match of the Day was covering that afternoon. Everyone expected Newcastle to win—except a close friend of mine, Ricky George, a former Barnet player. I'd known Ricky when I was a reporter on the local Barnet paper and we'd grown into close friends who would see each other socially.

In fact to this day we are friends—but that's sidetracking. Rick had joined Hereford. He was the ideal person to tell me all about the Hereford players.

On the Friday before the match Rick drove me down to Hereford to join the team. He was only chosen as substitute for the Cup tie so we went out for a meal the night before the match.

Late on we were introduced to Jackie Milburn and he told Rick that if he had been in his team— even as substitute—he would have gone to bed early and not been allowed out for a late night meal.

Rick replied that he'd show the night hadn't done any harm by scoring the winning goal! At the time it seemed a wild dream.

Newcastle were winning one-nil when Ronnie Radford hit a tremendous shot from the middle of the park that was to become the goal of the season.

Rick came on in extra time and, would you believe it, scored the winning goal! So I ended up interviewing Rick as the man who had caused one of the biggest upsets in F.A. Cup history.

We drove back to Barnet and had our own little celebration. Rick was drinking to his famous goal while I was rejoicing that my first F.A. Cup tie led off that night's Match of the Day programme.

I never expected to get a story out of the game—and there I was interviewing a mate who'd helped make Cup history!

John recounts that match eagerly. But his memories of his first-ever *Match of the Day* broadcast are not so sweet.

It was on Saturday, October 9, 1971. Another big crowd—48,464 —crowded into Anfield to see if Liverpool could preserve their unbeaten record against Chelsea.

My commentary was as bad as the match—a dreadful 0-0 draw. I wasn't petrified before the match because I had been commentating on radio. But I got the biggest shock of my life when I realised the difference between radio and television, and it took me three years before I felt I had made the transition.

For commentators their nightmare game would be having to report on a match between two non-league sides . . . played in Belgrade!

The secret of identification is experience—watching the same players over and over again. If it's Liverpool against Manchester United I should know the 22 players or I shouldn't be in the job. But when I have to go to watch a Third, Fourth Division or non-league team it's not so easy. I try to watch them training but if that isn't possible try to get a cassette or recording of them and watch it time after time.

The worst game I've had to do in that respect was a European Championship semi-final between West Germany and Yugoslavia in Belgrade.

I flew over the day before and had no opportunity to see the teams. The match was being played in a stadium which any commentator will tell you has the commentary position further away from the ground than any other in the world. It's right at the back of the stands, which are typically continental. The far touchline looks as though it's on another planet and the players look like matchstick men.

You can't identify the players from that distance, and all I had in front of me was a black and white monitor!

In Focus  Andy Gray

Winning the tackle is John Rowlinson.

When Tony Gubba chats away about *Match of the Day* he doesn't mean the Saturday night show that's compulsive viewing for millions.

It could be a Sunday afternoon game in front of a couple of hundred.

For off-screen Tony is organiser of a flourishing soccer side that includes several of his *Match of the Day* colleagues.

They tour the country, playing most Sundays against sides made up of ex-managers or local celebrities—with proceeds going to a worthy charity.

Throughout the winter months the *Match of the Day* side—its powerful half back is commentator John Motson, the show's producer John Rowlinson is a midfield dynamo, and trying to stop the opposition from scoring is floor manager Chris Lewis—turns up come hail, snow or sunshine for ninety minutes of action—the like of which you will never see on the programme.

They take their soccer seriously on *Match of the Day* and their team—augmented by occasional guest appearances from Brigh-

Is action better

John Motson lays off a square ball.

ton's Teddy Maybank, Hereford United's Peter Mellor (usually wearing a number nine shirt), ex-Scotland keeper Bob Wilson and other BBC sports personnel—has a growing reputation.

Such is their professionalism that they will even turn out at full-strength the week before the Cup Final!

Tony, who plays a vital role in the back four: "We love our football and there's no better way to spend a Sunday than out on the park.

"I like to think we are quite a good side. Besides helping keep us fit it gives pleasure to a lot of people."

For 32-year-old Motson, who spends his life describing the skills of the world's top players, it's an ideal opportunity to make up for his mis-spent youth.

He admitted: "I went to school in Suffolk where you played either rugby or hockey. There was no football at all at the school so I've tried to play as often as I could since leaving."

Half-time, and instead of a tactical talk from the manager, it's a quick sip of tea!

than words...

Match of the Day line-up. Left to right: John Rowlinson (studio director), Radio Sports Unit's Alan Parry, John Motson, Tony Gubba and floor manager Chris Lewis.

MATCH OF THE DAY

Date	Main Match	Commentator	Score	HT	Referee	Notes
5/2/12	Ipswich v Leeds	John Motson	5-1			

DIARY 1979

Second Match	Commentator	Score	HT	Referee	Notes
Man City v Bristol	Barry Davies				

The Editors would like to thank *Match of the Day* Editor Jonathan Martin and Series Producer Alec Weeks and their production teams for their help and assistance.

Editors: **Alan Kingston and Peter Oakes**
Designer: **Peter Corri**